John,
I wish you great

M000251362

wHolistic Change[SM]: Delivering Corporate Change That Lasts

Michelle Smeby and Patty Stolpman

John,
Best wishes and warm regards
for the future!

Patty Stolpman

Library of Congress Catalog Number: 2013942866

ISBN: 0615786588
ISBN-13: 978-0-615-78658-2

1. Organizational change. 2. Leadership

First Edition Printed in the United States of America

DEDICATION

Dedicated to change agents everywhere. We wish you success!

CONTENTS

MICHELLE SMEBY AND PATTY STOLPMAN

WHY WE WROTE THIS BOOK
AND WHAT WE HOPE YOU GET OUT OF IT

This book *had* to be written. Somebody had to do it. Too many change efforts have self-destructed. Sure, there are many books and articles about the theory of change and leading change, but we wanted a pragmatic, clear, concise methodology that we could use to actually achieve change.

The wHolistic Change℠ approach was developed over our combined 40 years of experience delivering successful corporate change. All aspects of the methodology have been tested at numerous Fortune 500 companies and vetted by conducting lessons learned and continuously improving the process.

If you are reading this book, you are considering or have already been assigned to play a role in a change effort. Change happens because of people: People create your products, people serve your customers, people develop new ways to bring in revenue, people choose to work for your company or to leave to go work somewhere else. When it is time to change, you must consider the impact of the change on the people in your organization.

Throughout this book, we provide information about change agents and the skills they'll need to be effective; how to overcome resistance to change; and decision points to determine if your team is prepared to deliver a corporate change that will truly last.

Historical Approaches to Change

Historical approaches to organizational change have tended to fall into two categories. The first is executive mandate, where leadership of a company decides on a change and directs the employees to conform.

Figure 1. Executive mandate: Leadership directs employees to conform.

The second category, which is less frequent, is the grass-roots movement, where the employees themselves see a need and come together to advocate for change.

Both of these approaches have their limitations. Executive mandate often achieves corporate compliance—with a human cost. Grass-roots organizing can achieve some degree of change. However, without senior leadership support, the chances are good that the employees will become exhausted and disillusioned. The change won't get very far.

Figure 2. Grass-roots movement: Employees advocate for change.

We offer an alternative approach to driving corporate change: Leaders driving change involve their employees in the process. They consider the impacts of their decisions on the welfare and engagement of their employees during and after the change process. This is why we created wHolistic Change℠. Our focus is on setting up employees, as well as their companies, for success.

Figure 3. wHolistic Change℠: Strong executive sponsorship with employee engagement.

The wHolistic Change℠ Framework

What differentiates wHolistic Change℠ is a pragmatic approach to change based on a framework described by four elements: services, people, process, and technology:

- Services are key for understanding change.

- People are the key to the success of that change.

- Process depicts how people and services come together to deliver the change.

- Technology includes the tool(s) that enable it all.

We refer to the services, people, process, and technology elements as the "quadrants."

Everything a person in your organization does is a service in some way: providing in-home appliance repair, picking merchandise for a customer order, developing software, handling customer-support calls, balancing the accounting ledgers.

Services	People
What services or products does your organization deliver—both to external and internal customers?	Who provides the services or products?
Process	**Technology**
When, where, and why do the services or products fit into your organization?	What tools are used in order to provide the services or products?

Figure 4. The wHolistic Change℠ quadrants.

When you need your people to do something different, the services they provide are changing. We believe that if change is planned around this understanding of services, with sensitivity to the people in your organization and a clear definition of the process and tools they'll use to provide the service, you will have established a path to success.

How We Have Organized This Book

Each chapter of this book is organized in the following way:

1. An explanation of the technique
2. Why the step is important to the methodology and what happens if you skip it
3. A checklist to apply the technique
4. A recap of the important points

Your change team will need people—men and women—to make the change a reality. Lacking a gender-neutral pronoun, we generically use "she" instead of "he or she" throughout the book.

We also use the generic term "organization." Please keep in mind that the wHolistic Change℠ techniques work whether the change you are making applies to a whole company, one division, or one department.

wHolistic Change℠ End-to-End

Although our approach lays out steps that fall into a logical sequence, it is important to note that change can be iterative. When everything goes according to plan, the sequence will pretty much flow from start to finish.

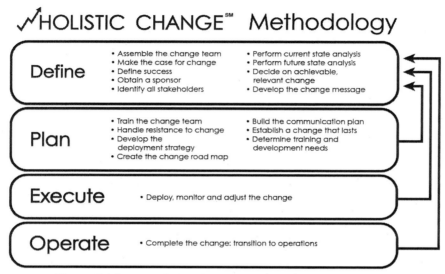

Figure 5. The wHolistic Change℠ end-to-end methodology.

Whenever you need to re-plan, change scope, or react to anything else that comes up, then jump back in at the appropriate step, make your adjustment, and move forward again from there.

Summary

This book lays out a pragmatic approach for defining, planning, and executing a change effort. It's intended to be a guide, giving you a framework and methodology to follow. We are not attempting to tackle the theory of change. For some of the literature that has helped inform our approach, please see the chapter entitled "Consulted References."

1 ASSEMBLE THE CHANGE TEAM

Explanation of the Technique

Implementing change doesn't happen with just one person. **It takes a team.** The wHolistic Change℠ methodology is based on a change team composition that has a set of defined roles, each with defined responsibilities:

1. Champion
2. Change agent
3. Change team manager
4. Communicator
5. Facilitator
6. Integrator
7. Owner and stakeholder
8. Sponsor
9. Subject matter expert

The change team will consist of employees who have proven credibility within the organization and who are viewed as subject matter experts (SMEs) in their areas. It will also include people who have demonstrated the ability to lead and drive organizational change. The goal is to create a self-sustaining change that will last after the core team of change agents disbands, which will happen once the change is operational.

Figure 6. Change requires a team.

Look throughout your organization to find the people with the right skills to fulfill the change team roles. It might be that one person covers multiple roles or that many people cover one role.

However the change team is formulated, make sure that there is somebody appointed to do each of these things and that everybody understands what is needed to satisfy her role.

It is **critical** to get skilled people assigned to your effort. Executives sometimes assign employees to change projects because those individuals can be "spared" from their regular duties. You need people with the capabilities to ensure a successful outcome. After you have the right people in the right roles, Chapter 10, "Train the Change Team," will explain the attitudes necessary to be a successful agent of change.

1. Champion

> *Champion:* an executive-level peer of the sponsor who has a vested interest in making sure the change succeeds. There will likely be resistance to change and barriers to adoption that your champion(s) will help you resolve. While this role is closely related to the sponsor role, champions are not on the hook to deliver the business value expected from the change.

The champion will be your positive voice to get people on board and excited about the change. This person may be an owner in the change effort; it may often be the sponsor who is also your biggest champion.

The champion must emphasize both her support for the initiative as well as the importance of the results to the organization. This will help to persuade people to get on board. Equally important are the champions in the trenches who will be able to laterally persuade their peers that change is actually a really good thing.

The key to a champion's effectiveness is her sphere of influence as well as her ability to inspire and motivate other people. Look for people to be champions whom their peers, their management, and their direct reports respect and who also have demonstrated the ability to influence people's behavior.

In some scenarios, the champion may have to mandate the change in order to get the desired result. This may be due to the speed of the change that is needed or to deal with an impacted group that is resisting. In general, mandating is not a desired approach, but recognize when it needs to be used and apply it sparingly.

2. Change agent

> *Change agent:* a person in the trenches who has the passion to make the change work and to maintain it long term.

A change agent is someone who is passionate about the vision for how the company will better serve its employees and customers after the change has taken place.

The change agent is able to define and act as an advocate for all of the following:

- The service changes: How the goods and services the company provides will change for the betterment of the company's customers.
- The people changes: What different skills will be needed to implement and then continuously operate in the changed world.
- The process changes: How what people do tomorrow will differ from what they do today.
- The technology change: What different tools will be used to meet the company's needs.

Change agents will be the early adopters of your new processes and/or technologies. They will be asked to help explain the change to the rest of the company.

These change agents will:

- Participate in template development.
- Provide examples.
- Conduct training.
- Encourage pilot participation.
- Build Communities of Practice among subject matter experts from across the company. (Communities of Practice will be discussed further in Chapter 5, "Identify All Stakeholders.")

In addition, change agents must be honest about what is working—and what is not—while staying positive about the need for the change.

For more information about change agents, see Chapter 10, "Train the Change Team."

3. Change team manager

> *Change team manager:* the project manager who will lead the change definition, change planning, and change execution, and who will wrap up the change effort by turning it over to operational business as usual.

Like any project, a change effort needs a good manager. There is a lot of excellent information explaining how to manage projects; our intent isn't to tell you **how to do** this role. Our intent is to tell you simply how important it is **to do** it.

If you don't have a strong manager, your odds of success drop dramatically.

The change team manager is the role that makes it all work. This person will be the public point of contact. She will shepherd the change effort through all of its twists and turns, issues and risks, and bring it through to success.

This role makes sure:

- There is a plan.
- Everything is going according to plan.
- Everything gets back on plan when there has been a bump in the road.

The change team manager actively manages the risks, issues, dependencies, and constraints, and makes sure that all of the other change team members are doing their jobs.

No matter what size the change effort might be, it requires thoughtfulness and planning. Even though your effort might be small, it is still important to name somebody as the change team manager. In a small effort, the same person might end up covering many of the change team roles and not be officially "titled" with those roles. Regardless of the size of the effort, the change team manager must be clearly identified.

For a large change effort, naming the change team manager is crucial. It provides everybody external to the effort—and more importantly, everybody being impacted by the change effort—a go-to person who will respond to her issues, questions, and concerns.

The change team manager must be aware of what the buzz is in the organization. She must make sure that any misinformation, miscommunication, misconceptions, and misunderstandings—anything that could potentially derail the success of the effort—get cleared up right away. This individual may need the communicator, sponsor, or champion to get the message out, but the change team manager makes sure the buzz gets back on track.

4. Communicator

Communicator: the person who will create and execute the communication plan. This is probably the most important role when it comes to making change successful and less painful for your employees.

You can never over-communicate!

One of the best techniques for making your change successful is to make sure that everybody knows what's going on—and why. This fosters a feeling of ownership and commitment from everybody involved.

Your communicator will make sure that each person impacted is informed and that she understands what her new world is going to look like.

If possible, your communicator should come from a marketing or communications background so she has a clear understanding of all the communication tools available. She will be able to recommend the most effective ways to communicate with everybody impacted by the change, both internal and external. In addition, she will know how to brand the messages so people start to recognize the change as they see it reinforced through multiple channels.

The communicator will ensure consistency of communications as she develops and manages the communication plan, which we will discuss in further detail in Chapter 14, "Build the Communication Plan."

5. Facilitator

> *Facilitator:* an individual who knows how to get everybody talking in an effective manner. This role helps people understand their common objectives and assists them to achieve consensus without taking a personal position. The facilitator will be called in, as needed.

When there are multiple people involved in and impacted by the change, making sure that everybody's voice is heard takes on huge importance. The facilitator's role is to make this happen.

The facilitator needs to reach out to all impacted parties, bring them together, and ensure that every person has an opportunity to state her point of view and her needs. Sometimes it can require detective work, cajoling, and mediation. It also requires asking the right questions and checking for understanding—all standard facilitation skills.

The facilitator will need to establish the ground rules that will be followed during discussion. Setting ground rules makes sure that everybody knows the expectations for how she will interact with everybody else, the right forums for bringing up topics, and how questions will be answered.

6

The facilitator also will define a decision-making protocol. Will the group make decisions by consensus? Will all parties have an equal voice? Or will there be a higher authority who makes the ultimate decision?

Clearly defining how decisions will be made will make sure nobody gets alienated because she feels she isn't being heard or she doesn't know how to get to a decision on a point she's raising.

The facilitator is the gatherer of information who works with all of the parties. Whatever the facilitator learns needs to be fed to the entire change team, especially the integrator and the communicator, to enable them to perform their roles.

The facilitator is also in a great position to first recognize risks and issues. Anything uncovered must be passed on to the change team—especially to the change team manager and sponsor—so that the risk or issue can be addressed as quickly as possible.

6. Integrator

> *Integrator:* the person who can take all of the different pieces and put them together into a whole that makes sense. The integrator role requires somebody who is a big-picture thinker who can also dwell in the details.

The facilitator makes sure that everybody's voice is heard, because each voice will have valuable information and her own perspective to contribute. The integrator will then take all of those separate voices and turn them into something whole.

The owners, change agents, and subject matter experts may represent disparate opinions and approaches. When that happens, the integrator will analyze each of the perspectives, identify the differences and commonalities, and determine if there's a solution that satisfies everybody's core needs. The integrator must be able to check for agreement across the stakeholders and ensure that what is being described works for everybody, both for the current state and the future state.

The perspective of the integrator has to be big picture and detailed at the same time. This requires a particular skill set. A person with a passion for solving puzzles and putting all of the pieces together makes a great integrator.

The integrator must be able to completely describe and document the change solution in such a way that people can understand what is changing in their daily lives. Think of it as providing a dictionary so that everybody can speak the same language regarding what the future will be. The integrator may want to engage the facilitator to manage the discussions when the future state proposal is reviewed with all of the impacted stakeholders in order to help achieve agreement.

The integrator provides the information about the change and the supporting visuals that the communicator needs to develop the appropriate communications.

7. Owner and stakeholder

> *Stakeholder:* a division or business entity that comprises one or more core business operations.

> *Owner:* an individual who is responsible for the business outcomes and day-to-day operations of the stakeholder. The owner will participate in the change effort planning and will govern the ongoing operations after the change is implemented.

The role names of stakeholder and owner are very close in meaning. When we look at the stakeholder analysis diagram in Chapter 5, "Identify All Stakeholders," we will try to identify all of the stakeholders—essentially, all of the impacted parties. Think of "stakeholder" in terms of impacted division or business entity from a general perspective.

For each stakeholder, a person needs to be identified as the owner. The owner will be the voice of that business operation, will be able to make decisions, and will be responsible for actively participating as a member of the change team. The owner has a lot to do with the success of the change effort.

An owner must make sure that:

- The facilitator has heard what she has to say.
- The integrator has fully understood what she needs and has included her needs in the big-picture definition.
- The communicator has gotten the message out to all of the stakeholder population.

- The sponsor has provided all of the resources—people, funding, hardware, software, and physical workspaces—needed.

- The owner has everything she needs to govern the ongoing operations after the change has happened.

When subject matter experts from inside the stakeholders are needed, the owner identifies the people with the right knowledge who can speak for her business unit. The owner also identifies the change agents from within her organization and assigns them to the change team.

The owner's role may be a bit different, depending on whether her stakeholder is on the receiving or the driving end of the change. Either way, the owner will be on the hook for advocating for her stakeholder's perspective, implementing the change, and making sure the change survives—and thrives.

8. Sponsor

> *Sponsor:* the executive who is the primary champion of the change. This individual will ensure that the needed resources are available: named individuals to participate in the change team, funding, hardware, software, and physical workspaces for the change team. The sponsor is on the hook to deliver the business value expected from the change.

Lining up an executive sponsor is the most critical step when tackling change. Your sponsor will be the name and face associated with the change and will be the key person to ensure that the change is successfully implemented.

The sponsor will be the person who will provide guidance in developing the change team, act as the escalation point as issues arise, and keep the momentum going through garnering excitement and celebrating the successes. The sponsor ultimately will be called upon to make critical decisions—up to employment-related decisions—when active resistance is encountered.

See also Chapter 4, "Obtain a Sponsor," and Chapter 11, "Handle Resistance to Change."

9. Subject matter expert

> *Subject matter experts (SMEs):* the individuals who know how their stakeholder develops products and services for their internal and external customers. To truly glean improvements from a change effort, you need a complete understanding of the current world and what your future world could be. Subject matter experts provide this.

The subject matter expert has the knowledge that you will need about the way things are right now and about the way things could be. You will need to understand both the current world and the future world in order to develop the plan for how to get to the change vision.

A subject matter expert can be someone internal to the organization or an expert from outside. Internal SMEs know your organization. They can help identify where things are really broken today and where the most future benefit can be achieved. A savvy internal SME will also be able to help you understand where the biggest pitfalls are hiding.

If you are talking to an internal SME, recognize that she is most likely being impacted by the change. A SME may be totally on board and one of your strongest change agents. These people are invaluable. Or she may think that everything is fine the way it is, thank you very much, and the SME may actually be a barrier to change.

It's going to be very important to understand her point of view. As you assess the information she's providing, you'll have to determine from what perspective she is offering her feedback. Is she in favor of or against the change?

If the vision you're setting out to achieve has already been implemented successfully somewhere else, you might want to bring in an external subject matter expert to save both time and money. You can use that person's experience to avoid missteps and to avoid having to reinvent the future world.

One caveat about external SMEs: Make sure the person you're working with understands that she is bringing her background and experience to the table but that she needs to really listen and understand what your organization needs.

The facilitator and integrator will work very closely with the subject matter experts. SMEs are the source of knowledge that will make the change successful.

Why Is This Step Important? What Happens if You Skip It?
It requires a team to make change happen. In order for your change to be successful, recognize that you will need to involve individuals from across your organization and potentially from outside the company to make the change a reality.

When you are looking for the right people to be involved on the change team, look for institutional knowledge. You need to know where this resides, because it can both benefit and hinder your efforts.

Recognize the positives of having people with significant institutional knowledge involved with your change effort. They can:

- **Help you figure out** how to get from here to there. Their knowledge of the organization as it is today will be invaluable in understanding your current world. It's from this basis that you'll be able to figure out who all of the impacted stakeholders are, what current communication channels exist, and which ones reach the people you need to connect with most effectively.

- **Navigate the pathways** of the organization. Their connections to and knowledge of the true power brokers (official or unofficial) can make or break you. Identify everybody who will need to be persuaded to be a champion or change agent for you. An organizational chart doesn't always give you the whole picture.

- **Point out hidden "gotchas"**. Institutional experts have been around for a while, so they can tell you why prior efforts have failed. What were the factors that caused something to fail? What were the reasons that something succeeded?

- **Tell you whom you need** to get on board. The people with institutional knowledge will know the people who are effective at getting a job done; they may be one of those individuals themselves. Find out whom they recommend you enlist.

Recognize that somebody with institutional knowledge has the potential to derail your efforts. For all of the same reasons she can help you, she also has the knowledge to go around behind you and cause you to fail. Make sure you know where she stands.

We have seen people join change efforts because they have opinions about what needs to be done in the organization; the launch of a change project is a chance to make it happen. These people's opinions about what needs to change may have been formed over many, many years. Maybe they are effective. Or they might be narrow-minded, might hijack the change to deliver a pet project, or might ignore root cause.

It can be dangerous if you do not set the expectations upfront and actively manage the roles and responsibilities of the members of the change team.

If your organization has struggled with change in the past, see if the root cause was insufficient resources—people, funding, hardware, software, or physical workspaces. Changes fail when people are expected to make change happen "off the sides of their desk, in their spare time."

Understanding the root cause of previous failures may provide the impetus to senior management that the investment in resources will be worth it to create a change that *truly* lasts.

Checklist

#	Role	Skill Set
1	Champion	• Develop strategy • Influence across business units • Improve business processes • Align core operations with corporate mission and strategic vision
2	Change agent	• Influence without authority • Improve business processes • Think critically, including exceptions • Understand interdependencies between business units • Understand core operations
3	Change team manager	• Understand project management • Develop and manage project plans • Possess Lean and/or Six Sigma analytic skills • Think critically, including exceptions • Develop and manage budgets • Plan deployments • Lead a project team • Manage issues and risks • Report status • Communicate with business and technical audiences
4	Communicator	• Understand internal and external communications planning • Develop branding such as logos, color scheme • Understand communication tools available • Develop and manage ongoing communication plans
5	Facilitator	• Possess facilitation expertise: establishing ground rules, asking questions, consensus building, clarifying for understanding, mediation • Coordinate inter- and intradepartmental brainstorming • Communicate with business and technical audiences • Identify and communicate issues and risks

#	Role	Skill Set
6	Integrator	• Elicit, capture, and clearly document business needs • Capture, document, analyze, and improve business processes • Possess Lean and/or Six Sigma analytic skills • Think critically, including exceptions • Understand interdependencies between business units • Understand core operations
7	Owner	• Understand and manage P&L statement(s) • Be responsible for one or more core operations • Develop business benefits • Develop technical benefits • Define and manage core operational processes, techniques, roles and responsibilities, and templates used by practitioners • Set guidelines and standards • Train core operations and ensure certifications • Govern proficiency and compliance of core operations • Improve business processes • Align core operations with corporate mission and strategic vision
8	Sponsor	• Develop P&L statement(s) • Develop corporate strategy • Influence across business units • Improve business processes • Align core operations with corporate mission and strategic vision
9	Subject matter expert	• Possess industry expertise and/or expertise in the change being implemented • Understand interdependencies between business units • Understand core operations

Figure 7. The change team roles and skill sets needed.

Recap of the Technique

Implementing change doesn't happen with just one person, it takes an entire team. The change team will be composed of employees who have proven credibility within the organization, plus individuals who have demonstrated the ability to lead and drive organizational change.

The goal in assembling the change team is to identify the people who will create a self-sustaining change that will live on after the change team disbands. This will happen once the change is operational.

We start by describing the roles and responsibilities of the various people who will make up your change team. The actual naming and assembling of the change team will happen as you determine success, perform stakeholder analysis, and identify the internal and external stakeholders who will be affected by your change.

You may find that there are people who are assigned to the change team who are uncomfortable playing the roles to which they were assigned.

As we will emphasize in Chapter 10, "Train the Change Team," the majority of the members of the change team will need to act as change agents within your organization. If an individual is not able to fulfill her role, work with your sponsor to identify the right replacement.

Poor attitudes can undermine a project. Your organization's attitude about the change starts with the change team.

2 MAKE THE CASE FOR CHANGE

Explanation of the Technique

wHolistic Change℠ defines change as transitioning from what people do today to what you want them to do tomorrow. There are four critical questions to ask in order to understand the motivations for the change and what your organization hopes to get out of it:

1. What is the business problem or opportunity?
2. Who wants to change?
3. Why do they want a change?
4. How will the change benefit the person or organization who wants it? Why would the change be a good thing?

Ask stakeholders at all levels of the organization these questions. Their answers will vary, based on their perspectives, and all stakeholders' answers will need to be considered to determine the right change path forward.

1. What is the business problem or opportunity?

There are many reasons that change needs to happen. A foundational aspect is that the core values of the individual or the organization are not being met.

Core values may be explicitly stated as goals, a vision, or a mission statement, and so on. Values may also be implicit—characteristics of the culture of the organization. The intent of change is to better our organizations in both tangible and intangible ways.

Figure 8. The case for change: What is the motivation for change and what does your organization hope to get out of it?

As the business problem or opportunity for the organization is being defined, put thought into whether or not the goals are something that an individual can grab onto, make her own, and claim proud ownership of. Aligning personal goals with organizational goals gives you built-in change agents.

2. Who wants to change?

Change that is sustainable and that achieves a goal really begins from the hearts of people who are looking for something better. This can be anybody in your organization: the assembly-line worker who has an ingenious idea on how to improve performance on the line, the executive leadership team members who are dedicated to moving the organization forward in their market, or anyone in between.

Understanding *who* wants to change is important in order to make sure that you've asked the following questions of the right people.

3. Why do they want a change?

If the status quo were good, you probably wouldn't be looking to change. When talking to the stakeholders, ask "why" enough times until you feel you've really discovered the root of the stakeholders' needs or concerns.

Asking "why" also helps you discover how the stakeholders think they can contribute. If you can use their ideas and their energy, and let them lead pieces of the change, their personal motivation will be aligned with the organization's motivation.

Understanding the reasons and motivations for change will help you do a much better job of communicating to everybody why you are making the change.

Here are some motivations to consider:

- **Basic survival** of your company. If you're in a competitive environment and the only way you can continue to be a viable organization is to adapt and provide the new thing that your customers are looking for, then you change or you die.

- Recognition that your company is OK where it is in your market. However, **you can't grow** and you can't expand without making some kind of change. This motivation is beyond survival of the moment and is all about the ability to grow.

- Your company is already at the top of the game competitively. Still, there is **room for improvement** in your market and there are up-and-coming competitors who could knock you out of the top position. Your motivation is to continue to strive for excellence.

- The company is doing well competitively, yet **employee satisfaction** is at an **all-time low**. This motivation is more about the people and process aspects of change than about the services or technology aspects. Because you are unable to attract and retain talented employees, it's hurting your overall prospects for the future. Ultimately, this impacts your long-term survival and your ability to grow.

- Your company is doing well competitively. It is the company's culture, vision, and/or mission to be **innovative** and to seek new products or improvements to process. You want to not only survive but to thrive.

4. How will the change benefit the person or organization who wants it?

Usually part of the "why" a change is wanted has to do with benefits that are being sought. Ask your stakeholders "why" enough times to be able to articulate the expected benefits that will result from making the change.

Why Is This Step Important? What Happens if You Skip It?

There is a human problem behind any business problem. Unless you correct the human component, you will never truly solve the issue. Before your company revamps the services you provide to your customers, reorganizes the people, changes existing processes, or invests in new technology, make sure that you truly understand the cause—not just the symptom—for why you need to change.

In order to get to the root cause of why your organization needs to change, interview stakeholders to get to the heart of their pain points and what they value.

Checklist

#	Question	Clarifying Commentary	Stakeholder Response
1	What is the business problem or opportunity?	Stakeholder need or concern	The surface of the Lincoln Memorial was deteriorating due to frequent washing.
2	Who is asking for change?	Stakeholders (internal and external)	National Park Service
3	Why #1	Why is change important? Why is the problem happening?	Why was the memorial being washed so often? To remove all the pigeon guano.
4	Why #2	Why …?	Why were there so many pigeons? The pigeons ate the large number of spiders.
5	Why #3	Why …?	Why were there so many spiders? The spiders ate the high number of gnats.
6	Why #4	Why …?	Why were there so many gnats? The gnats were attracted to the lights on the memorial.
7	Why #5	What is the heart, or true systemic cause, of the business problem or opportunity?	Why were there more gnats at the Lincoln Memorial than at other sites? Traditionally, the lights at the Lincoln Memorial have been turned on at sunset, while the lights at other memorials are turned on an hour after sunset.
8	How will change benefit the stakeholder?	What's in it for them?	Turning the lights on at the Lincoln Memorial an hour after sunset will reduce the gnats, spiders, and pigeons and thus the need for frequent washing with harsh detergents. This will preserve the memorial.

Figure 9. Five whys case for change worksheet, including an example.

Recap of the Technique

The most important first step in approaching change is to understand why you need to change and to have thought through the business value that change is expected to deliver.

Once you have interviewed your stakeholders and have an idea of their motivations for change, you can start to quantify what successful change will look like.

3 DEFINE SUCCESS

Explanation of the Technique

At the outset of embarking on a wHolistic Change℠ effort, you must be able to describe what success looks like. This allows you to know if you are making progress toward the goal, to quantify the progress, and to identify opportunities to adjust if the goal is not being achieved.

There are three questions that will help you to know if you've achieved successful change:

1. How will you measure success?
2. What will the change look like once it is implemented?
3. How will you know that change has actually happened?

1. How will you measure success?

After understanding why you want or need to make a change and what the expected benefits are, how will you know if you've been successful?

Think about how you answered the question "How will the change benefit the stakeholder who wants it?" when you were laying out the case for change. What are some of the ways that you could objectively measure if you're getting the benefit you want?

If no objective measurement is possible, is there a subjective method that will give you an answer instead? If you really want an objective measure and none exists, your change effort will have to include putting a measurement method in place.

Figure 10. Define success: What is the measurable goal?

Think about the long-term view when you're defining what successful change looks like. The strength of the leadership and sponsorship is hugely important to being able to keep on course when other people think you're taking too long. If the change effort is expected to take a long time, try to establish some interim achievement points that can be used as success measurement milestones.

For long-term change, an attitude of planting a seed, nurturing it, and remaining flexible gives you a better opportunity to recognize issues and make course adjustments as needed, while still staying in tune with the original vision.

2. What will the change look like once it is implemented?
We'll talk more later about describing the future vision. Essentially, you need to be thinking about what operational changes will be apparent. Will you be producing a new product? Will your employees be taking on new responsibilities? Will your organizational structure be modified? Will an old operation be shut down?

What are the nonoperational changes that you are looking for? These aren't as easy to describe, but here are some examples:

- Are you looking for increased employee participation in an organizational program?
- Are you looking for a better response on an annual survey regarding how your employees feel about the organization?
- Are you looking for improved employee retention statistics?

3. How will you know that change has actually happened?
Proving that change has actually occurred can be done using measurements taken before and after the change. The measurements you take to determine success will provide an objective indication that change actually happened. When you consider what your measurements are, identify concrete things that are capable of being measured.

When your organization has metrics embedded in current organizational management, then your job becomes easier when you say your objective is to improve from current performance on one of those metrics. Having a metric to work from also gives your change more credibility and a common understanding to work with in discussion with leadership.

When what you are changing is harder to measure because it's a goal that is not as easily quantified, look for other things in the organization that are measured and that can give you an indication of success.

Examples are as follows:

- You see an improved reputation in the marketplace because your customer service center is spending more time on customer support.
- The number of applicants for an open job position is trending up because you are now an employer of choice.

Why Is This Step Important? What Happens if You Skip It?
We don't just include the definition of success because Michelle is a geeky engineer who loves math!

Concrete metrics help remove the emotional and personal reactions to change. It changes the conversation from what can be perceived as a personal attack on an owner to an objective business conversation about current state and where you need to go as an organization.

Checklist

#	Question	Clarifying Commentary	Stakeholder Response
1	What is the business problem or opportunity?	Business driver for change	Too many defects in the current process causing rework
2	Who is asking for change?	Stakeholders (internal and external)	Product quality assurance team
3	What is the vision?	How will the business look after the change?	Rework avoided
4	How will success be measured?	Measurement	(Cost in $ to reprocess the product) x (number of products that need to be reprocessed)
5		Mechanism to measure the change	Quarterly product quality report
6	What will change look like after it is implemented?	Current state	$100/unit x 1 million units/quarter x 20% defect rate
7		Future state goal	$100/unit x 1 million units/quarter x 15% defect rate
8		Timing when future state is expected to be achieved	Q4

Figure 11. Define success metrics checklist, including an example.

Recap of the Technique

In order to know whether you actually achieved change, you need to be able to describe what success is.

Quantifying change in business terms enables you to know if you are making progress toward the goal and the rate of that progress, as well as to identify opportunities to adjust if the goal is not being achieved.

4 OBTAIN A SPONSOR

Explanation of the Technique

As we said earlier, your sponsor will be the name and face associated with the change. A wHolistic Change℠ sponsor provides guidance in developing the change team, acts as the escalation point as issues arise, and keeps the momentum going through garnering excitement and celebrating the successes. The sponsor will be called upon to make critical decisions—up to employment-related decisions—when active resistance is encountered.

As an executive within your organization, your sponsor will also be able to align the change effort with the overall strategy, mission, and vision of your company in order to help others see the importance and business value of change.

When the change gets underway, how will you keep spirits up in the face of resistance? How will you handle what appears to be either outright hostility to the change you're trying to implement or back-room maneuvering that seems to have a goal of undermining the direction you're heading?

Figure 12. The sponsor: Executive who is on the hook to deliver the business value expected from the change.

Here's what a sponsor can do:

- Find ways to **nurture** your change agents. After a really stressful meeting, for example, a sponsor can tell the change team to take a break and do something relaxing. Invite them to take a walk outside if your workplace is in an environment conducive to that, send them to get a cup of coffee outside of your building, or assign them a short task that they can do well and successfully.

- Make sure that the change agents are **recognized** for the efforts they're making—to their peers, their management, and, if appropriate, to the whole organization.

- Be a **sounding board** for the change team manager. Everybody needs to talk through things once in a while.

- Most importantly, **support the change agents** and back them up. When the change team has to handle resistance to change, ask the sponsor to help. The sponsor can leverage her connections to determine why certain stakeholders are resisting and find creative ways to get them on board. The sponsor may be able to retool the change message to be more impactful with a particular audience. The sponsor may even be able to convince an owner to participate on a limited basis or on a small project to prove out the change before impacting an entire business unit.

- Yield the **heavy hammer** and require the organization to participate in the change. The sponsor's role as a respected executive gives you some weight to throw around; recognize when it's really needed. Because this behavior is how executive mandates drive change, we recommend you use this option sparingly—and only as a last resort.

Why Is This Step Important? What Happens if You Skip It?

Given how important executive sponsorship is to the success of a change effort, what should you do if you cannot secure—or if you lose—your sponsor?

1. Identify an **alternate** executive to become your sponsor:
   - Find someone else who is respected within the organization and who is willing to support the need for change. Ensure that this executive understands and is willing to combat the resistance that the change will encounter.
   - Make sure to explain the role of the sponsor and the amount of time this person will spend making it a reality.
2. If #1 is not successful, determine if you feel the change is important enough to **forgo a sponsor** and to champion it as a grass-roots movement:
   - Be prepared for the fact that the change will take longer to implement without a sponsor because you will need to convince every impacted stakeholder, person by person.
   - Ensure that the change agents are prepared to put in more hours on the change. Such things as the communication plan, status reporting, and overcoming resistance to change will require additional evidence from the change team. Smaller, incremental successes will be required to establish credibility and to get more people to be willing to test the approach.
   - Create the change road map (see Chapter 13, "Create the Change Road Map") so that you have a clear understanding of timing for specific achievements and so that you are tracking your project status accordingly. This may help mitigate the change team becoming disheartened or burned out by showing

them that progress is being made, just very slowly and over a prolonged period of time.

3. If #1 and #2 do not work, review the case for change that prompted the creation of the project and determine whether the answers that drove the original rationale for change still apply:

   o What is the business problem or opportunity?

   o Who wants to change?

   o Why do they want the change?

   o How will the change benefit the person or organization who wants it?

   o If no executive is willing to sponsor it, how might people within the organization (negatively) interpret the change?

4. If the change is still valid, use the answers to #3 in a candid discussion with your former sponsor or a potential new executive sponsor about why you need her to publicly support the change.

5. If the answers to #3 are no longer valid, if the answers have materially changed due to internal or external factors or due to market conditions, or if you still cannot get a sponsor, determine if the best course of action is to cancel the initiative and redeploy the team:

   o Do not view canceling the change as a failure. See it as a business decision in the context of what is going on in your organization and how much and what types of change the organization can absorb at this time.

   o Involve the champions and the rest of the change team in the decision process in order to make the call together about canceling the project. Talk through the schedule, budget, and people commitment necessary to achieve change. Determine whether the project can truly achieve the defined success.

   o Perform a formal project closure:

     ▪ Communicate the decision to everybody involved in the change. Ensure that all stakeholders understand the rationale for stopping the project at this time.

     ▪ Conduct a "lessons learned" to see if there are improvements that could be leveraged, even if the complete end-to-end change is not implemented.

     ▪ Update all documentation associated with the change and archive it. If a sponsor and a business case for doing a similar change arise in the future, the materials can be used as launching-off points for the next change team.

Checklist

#	Sponsor Candidate Questions
1	How committed is she to the change?
2	Is she willing to send communications and visibly demonstrate her dedication to the change? Will she use her political clout to ensure a successful deployment across the organization?
3	Will she fund or help obtain funding, as needed, to support the change?
4	Will she chair a steering committee of peers to gain additional executive support for the change and to ensure that you are not a lone voice in a sea of passivity or resistance?
5	Has she ever acted as a change sponsor before? If not, you may need to train your sponsor to ensure that she is prepared for her role and what it means.

Figure 13. Questionnaire for assessing executives to become your sponsor.

Decision Point: Sponsorship?

If an executive sponsor is missing from your change initiative, STOP NOW! Without strong sponsorship, you will only frustrate people and not successfully deploy the change.

Recap of the Technique

No matter how obvious the need to change is, we guarantee that you will encounter resistance. When the change starts to roll out, there must be an executive who will stand up in front of the organization and who will champion, explain, and drive the need for change.

This sponsor must be willing to stand firm when middle-level management, those most affected by the change, escalate to their leadership all of the reasons why they cannot possibly adopt this change at this time.

5 IDENTIFY ALL STAKEHOLDERS

Explanation of the Technique

Too often people in corporations focus on their part of the world rather than thinking about the larger organization or broader business environment. Successful changes are inclusive; successful changes take place across the organization—not in a silo.

A wHolistic Change℠ tool that can be a handy device for understanding the depth, breadth, and control of a change is something we call a **stakeholder analysis**. This is a simple visual that shows all stakeholders involved in and impacted by the change you're tackling, including stakeholders both internal and external to your organization.

Figure 14 shows an example for an effort that will be rolling out a new product to the company's customers.

The stakeholders depicted with vertical boxes are the organizational entities that own a particular aspect of the change. The stakeholders depicted with horizontal boxes have a span of control that extends beyond just one of the vertical organizational entities—usually some form of governance.

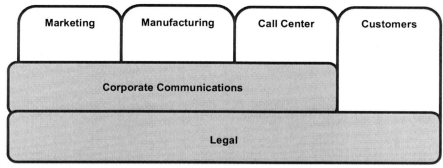

Figure 14. Stakeholder analysis: Identify all stakeholders that are involved in or impacted by the change.

The stakeholder analysis visual is a great communication tool to gain an understanding of the involvement needed by everybody impacted by the change:

- Will she be an active part of the change effort?
- Will she need to govern what is changing?
- Will she simply need to be kept informed about what is happening?

For each identified stakeholder, name the **owner**. The owner must be empowered to make decisions, and she will be expected to deliver the change within her business operation. The owners will name the change agents and subject matter experts who will participate in the current state and future state analysis, as well as the Communities of Practice (CoPs) and change planning activities that follow.

In order to establish a change that lasts, involve the people impacted by the change in the process.

Communities of Practice are networks of people who are focused on a common interest, supporting each other's development and growth. By participating in a Community of Practice, community members exchange ideas, collaborate, and learn from one another. Members identify best practices, develop expertise, and access a constant flow of information to do their jobs better and more consistently.

Communities can be managed in a variety of ways, such as facilitated meetings, suggestion boxes, wikis, or social software. We will talk more about CoPs in Chapter 15, "Establish a Change That Lasts."

Why Is This Step Important? What Happens if You Skip It?

When you identify impacted stakeholders, the ideal scenario is to have each stakeholder identify a named person to represent her area as the operational owner. The owner will be responsible for implementing the change and for ongoing business operations.

Figure 15. Without stakeholder analysis, a small group decides in a silo what changes need to be made.

The owner of each stakeholder will be included in the formulation and planning of the change. This person should have valuable information at her fingertips about how to implement new processes or technology within her department.

Owners need to weigh in on whether or not the current staff members have the needed skills or if they'll need training to be ready for their new responsibilities. Owners can identify whether or not current staffing levels will support what they are being asked to do, if additional people will be needed, or if current staffing levels can be decreased as a result of the change.

One caveat: We recommend engaging your Human Resources (HR) department when performing the stakeholder analysis. HR is tasked with understanding the makeup of your organization's workforce and determining the skills and qualifications of that workforce. While the owners may have a gut feel for what will be needed in terms of their staff,

Human Resources will be able to make the official determination of staffing levels, training, and development.

If you do not perform stakeholder analysis, a small group may decide in a silo on the change needed. This team will act without a broader understanding of the impact of the change on the people who will be affected. This could cause at best cross-departmental friction and delays, while impacted stakeholders struggle to figure out what they need to do to deliver their component of the change. At worst, it could lead to executive escalation and killing of the change effort.

Checklist

To identify all stakeholders affected by your change, look in particular for intersections and handoff points between departments. This will become especially important for developing the change road map in Chapter 13, "Create the Change Road Map." You will need to know what other changes are being implemented within the vertical and horizontal practices across the corporation.

#		Stake-holder	Owner	SME(s)	Change Agent(s)
Vertical Stakeholder Characteristics					
1	Own a particular core operation or organizational entity				
2	Define all aspects of their practice: processes, techniques used, roles and responsibilities, guidelines, and standards				
3	Develop and maintain templates used by their practitioners				
4	Determine technology that will best enable their practice				
5	Develop and maintain training for the practice, up to and including certifications of proficiency				
6	Govern proficiency and compliance of practitioners with respect to the practice				
7	Continuously improve the practice				
8	Set strategic message for their organizational entity and ensure alignment with the overall corporate mission and vision				

#		Stake-holder	Owner	SME(s)	Change Agent(s)
Horizontal Stakeholder Characteristics					
9	Have a span of control that extends beyond just one of the vertical organizational entities— usually some sort of governance or quality assurance				
10	May provide a service to a vertical stakeholder, for example, Information Services providing the technology chosen for use by a department or Project Management ensuring the development of a product from concept through to customer delivery				
11	Ensure that a decision by one vertical stakeholder does not break the handoffs to other stakeholders; facilitate communication across vertical stakeholders				
12	Govern proficiency and compliance of practitioners with respect to the practice				
13	Continuously improve the practice				

#		Stake-holder	Owner	SME(s)	Change Agent(s)
14	Set the strategic message for their organizational entity and ensure alignment with the overall corporate mission and vision				

Figure 16. Stakeholder analysis guidelines and checklist.

Recap of the Technique

Stakeholder analysis enables you to understand everything upstream and downstream from each point of change. It also enables you to quantify the services, people, processes, and technology that will be impacted. This effort will lead you to a current state definition.

When each organizational unit identified on the stakeholder analysis provides named individuals to participate in planning and executing the change, you are starting to put together the change picture—from a wHolistic Change℠ perspective.

6 PERFORM CURRENT STATE ANALYSIS

Explanation of the Technique

When you start defining change, make sure you understand what your current world looks like. To move the organization from here to there, you have to know where "here" is.

Anecdotal evidence might have been the motivation for saying that a change was needed. How bad are things, really? Reality may be better—or worse—than you think. Is your vision really that different from where you are now? With the results of a current state analysis you will have a fact-based start to planning your change.

In the wHolistic Change℠ approach, there are four specific types of questions to ask, upfront, to ensure that your sponsor understands the type of change, magnitude, and speed at which she can expect to drive the change:

1. Services: What do the people do?
2. People: Who is changing?
3. Process: What is the context for what they do, and why?
4. Technology: What tools support them?

How you answer these questions will determine the efforts the deployment planning will spawn. All of the change management and communications will depend on the organization's decisions about how it wants to organize itself and whether it is willing to adjust the existing structure because of the change.

Figure 17. Current state: Where is your organization today?

One other important note: The questions in the current state checklist sound like they are driving toward an assessment for the entire organization. Actually, these same questions apply when you are looking at making a change within just one department.

Think of the specific area that you are looking to change as being "my organization" and look to the next level out from you as being your customer. Even if you are not providing services to a customer outside of your organization, every other area internal to your organization that uses what you provide is an internal customer. As a customer, she is of course as deserving of the same attention as an external customer.

Why Is This Step Important? What Happens if You Skip It?
When an organization recognizes that it is time to change, it is critically important to get the current world and future world right. If you do not have a clear, accurate portrayal of how the process actually works today, it is unlikely that any changes you make will truly reap all of the benefits you are trying to achieve.

There are often many documented process flows and procedures. Nevertheless, when you take the time to walk the process, you will find all of the undocumented steps people take or documented steps that are skipped. You might also uncover if anyone actually looked at the process flow showing how work is supposedly "done."

You also may find that there is a significant break in the current process. Correcting that issue alone may get you the business value you are trying to achieve. Sometimes huge initiatives are launched to solve relatively minor problems.

Checklist

#	Services Quadrant Current State Assessment
1	Who are all of our customers? Are they internal to the organization, or are they external?
2	For each of our customers, from *their* perspective: • What do we do for them? • What goods do they want to buy from us? • How do we make their lives better?
3	What kind of commitment have we made to our customers regarding the level of service we'll provide to them? Are there any variations by customer or by pricing structure?
4	How do our customers feel about the services or products that we are providing to them? Are they happy?
5	What does the business environment around our organization look like? How does it affect us?
6	Is the economic climate good? Or is it a concern right now?
7	Do we have the ability to operate in a free-market manner? Or do we have regulatory and other restrictions imposed on us?
8	What global changes in the next three years may impact the services we provide today?
9	Will changing demographics impact the demand for our services?

Figure 18. Services quadrant current state analysis questionnaire.

#	People Quadrant Current State Assessment
1	Who are the people we employ to provide the services? Are they all internal to the organization? Do we use contract resources or a mix?
2	What are the skills that our people have? Do they all have the same skills? Or do we have a mix of skills needed by different people?
3	Do our employees need training? Or are they all fully qualified for what we are expecting them to do?
4	Do our employees need to be certified in order to do their jobs?
5	Is innovation encouraged? Or is conformity more important?
6	Is our organization organized hierarchically with everything coming from the top and going down? Or is our organization more organic with units working together horizontally?
7	How does our organization approach diversity? Is it barely accepting, tolerating, or welcoming of diversity?
8	Is there a channel for suggestions to bubble up and will ideas be paid attention to? Are suggestions encouraged?
9	How do our people feel about their work lives? Are they happy? Or are they dissatisfied with their work lives? Do they feel like they are working in a safe environment and that they are valued for what they bring to our organization?
10	Do we have the authority to change our employees' job descriptions and job expectations?
11	Do our employees feel like they have work/life balance?

Figure 19. People quadrant current state analysis questionnaire.

#	Process Quadrant Current State Assessment
1	What do our current processes look like? Take the time to really analyze and understand the transition points in existing processes. In addition, analyze any alternate paths that the process can take, for example manufacturing lines, customer interactions, or product support. Gather information about processes that may be back-office functions such as finance, regulatory compliance, and so on.
2	Who participates in the processes? What does each person do?
3	What service or outcome does each process produce?
4	Where are the shortcomings? Where are the bottlenecks? Where are the places that we're losing quality?

Figure 20. Process quadrant current state analysis questionnaire.

#	Technology Quadrant Current State Assessment
1	What does our current technology look like to support our processes to deliver services? Technology can include manufacturing equipment, tools, or software, for example.
2	Is our existing technology adequate for the services we provide? If not, what are the gaps?
3	Is our current technology able to grow to support the three-year vision for the services we provide? If not, what are the gaps?
4	Are there any processes that we are doing completely manually, where there is technology that could support the process? Technology solutions could be packaged software, tools available in the market, or could be built in-house.
5	Is our technology a competitive advantage?
6	Is our technology no longer supported?

Figure 21. Technology quadrant current state analysis questionnaire.

Once you've answered the questions and gathered the information regarding your current world, analyze what you've learned.

Look for the interrelationships between aspects of each of the different categories of questions:

- Are your **processes** not able to deliver the **services** needed because the **technology** is outdated and doesn't allow you to keep up with your customers' desire?

- Is employee satisfaction at an all-time low because the **people** who are expected to do the **process** have not been trained for what they are being expected to do?

- Is your company's ability to offer innovative **services** limited because **people** don't believe suggestions are encouraged?

You get the idea. The ability to truly understand where you are comes from putting together all of the pieces of your current state.

Recap of the Technique

To move the organization from here to there, you have to know where "here" is.

Anecdotal evidence might have been the motivation for saying that a change was needed. However, only by performing a current state analysis will you have a clear and fact-based understanding of the state your organization is in. This will be the foundation upon which the future state analysis will be performed.

7 PERFORM FUTURE STATE ANALYSIS

Explanation of the Technique

What are your goals for the change? What does your world look like after the wHolistic Change℠ is implemented and your organization is performing? In the future state analysis, you put in writing what you expect in the future.

In the same way that you analyzed your current world, describe your future world according to the four quadrants:

1. Services: What are the services and/or products that your organization will provide?
2. People: What will your workforce look like?
3. Process: What will your processes look like?
4. Technology: What tools and systems will you use?

When you are describing your future, it will be important to understand the priority of each element. What is a "must have" and what is a "nice to have"? You will also want to understand any interconnection between the different elements. If one of the elements is a "must have," then any other element needed to achieve the first one also becomes a "must have."

For example, you are bringing a new product to market ("must have"). In order to provide the new service, you will need new technology and processes. You will need people who have been trained to use the new technology and processes to produce the product. An improvement in workforce satisfaction ("nice to have") may result from this, but you can still achieve your goal of bringing a new product to market without affecting change in workforce satisfaction.

Figure 22. Future state: In an ideal world, where does your organization want to be?

If workforce satisfaction is your "must have," then what are the other elements that will get you the required impact on satisfaction? Elimination of pain points? Culture changes? Better processes? Different technology?

Why Is This Step Important? What Happens if You Skip It?
Will the changes you want actually deliver the business expectations that drove the creation of this change effort? A key litmus test for your future state analysis is whether the future you are describing will achieve the case for change success metrics outlined in Chapter 3, "Define Success." If not, determine whether you are missing a key service, people, process, or technology that will enable you to deliver the expected outcomes in the timeframe specified.

We have seen organizations that lack consistent process, governance, and/or communication mechanisms. If the change effort does not address the process, governance, and/or communication gaps as part of the future state analysis, it will fail. In order to be successful the change must be established as part of how the company operates on a day-to-day basis.

Even if the change itself is a good idea, there is no guarantee that it will be embraced. The change must be incorporated into every aspect of how your company does business. It must be governed to ensure adoption and communicated—frequently, through multiple mechanisms—until the change becomes the way you do business.

Checklist

#	Services Quadrant Future State Assessment	Priority
1	Who will use the product or service?	Must Have / Nice to Have
2	Where will people use the product or service? Will it have any impacts on other people around them when they're using it?	Must Have / Nice to Have
3	What else has to be in place in order for our product or service to be usable, for example, power grid, highway system, or level of literacy?	Must Have / Nice to Have
4	Where will the materials come from geographically and from whom will we source them? How will materials be transported? Are they already in the right form? Or do they need processing before they're usable by us?	Must Have / Nice to Have
5	Will we make the product ourselves? Or will we have it made for us?	Must Have / Nice to Have
6	Who will quality check the product or service? Can it be done internally? Or will we need an external audit?	Must Have / Nice to Have
7	How will we get it to our customers? Is it something the customers can carry away themselves? Or will we need to provide some kind of delivery service?	Must Have / Nice to Have
8	At end of life, how will the product be disposed of? Is it toxic and therefore will require special handling? Is there an opportunity for reuse or recycling? Is there already an established reuse or recycling chain in place? Or will we need to develop one? With whom in the community will we need to work to make this happen?	Must Have / Nice to Have
9	Is what we're proposing governed by any agency or legal entity? Are there approvals we will need to secure before we can move forward with our plans?	Must Have / Nice to Have

#	Services Quadrant Future State Assessment	Priority
10	Are there public-interest groups that care about the domain into which we're trying to introduce our product or service? Will these groups be happy with our proposal?	Must Have / Nice to Have
11	How will using our new product or service change lives? Will something else stop being used? Who makes or provides that something else: our company or a competitor?	Must Have / Nice to Have
12	Are there key customer or market commitments that cannot be affected by the change? If there are specific high-profile deliverables that cannot afford to be missed, leadership may want to consider the timing of the change rollout and the timing for the specific people involved in these projects to adopt the change.	Must Have / Nice to Have

Figure 23. Services quadrant future state analysis questionnaire.

#	People Quadrant Future State Assessment	Priority
People Planning and Management		
1	Are we expecting more than one person or team can accomplish?	Must Have / Nice to Have
2	Are we asking for too many varied skills? Would it be really hard to find all of that experience in one person?	Must Have / Nice to Have
3	Are we asking for something so specialized that we will need to pay top salary to attract and retain that talent? This isn't necessarily a bad thing; it just needs to be worked into the cost benefit.	Must Have / Nice to Have
4	Will training work to bring our current team to the point where we need them? Or will we hire new people and train existing staff? Or will we just hire new people? How will we make that assessment?	Must Have / Nice to Have
5	What will the internal organization structure look like?	Must Have / Nice to Have
6	What is the expected organizational growth over the next three years (for example, 20% increase in full time employees)?	Must Have / Nice to Have
7	What is the right number of people, with the right skill sets, to provide the services expected?	Must Have / Nice to Have

#	People Quadrant Future State Assessment	Priority
8	In what state is the organization? How much change can be tolerated at one time?	Must Have / Nice to Have
9	Are there other major change initiatives being deployed concurrently? Consider the services, people, process, and technology impacts to all of the stakeholders and how their roles will need to change. Consider how this change will need to align with those initiatives.	Must Have / Nice to Have
Culture		
10	How will management value and reward employees' innovation and/or participation in change efforts, going forward?	Must Have / Nice to Have
11	How much time will be set aside for innovation and/or participation in Communities of Practice (CoPs)?	Must Have / Nice to Have
12	To whom will new ideas and continuous improvement suggestions be communicated?	Must Have / Nice to Have
13	Does our organization need training in collaboration? In innovation? In valuing diversity?	Must Have / Nice to Have
Personnel Development		
14	What will individual competency matrix and career paths look like?	Must Have / Nice to Have
15	What will organizational competency matrix and career paths look like?	Must Have / Nice to Have
16	Are job descriptions and compensation levels aligned with our industry to allow for our organization to be an employer of choice?	Must Have / Nice to Have
17	What skills will be needed in our organization? Perform current skills assessment such as individual assessments and group view aggregations of skills.	Must Have / Nice to Have
18	What training and development do our employees need? Develop individual development plans using the competencies, career paths, and training program.	Must Have / Nice to Have
19	What are the organization's certification goals?	Must Have / Nice to Have
20	How do individual incentives need to be refined to meet the development goals?	Must Have / Nice to Have

#	People Quadrant Future State Assessment	Priority
21	How are middle managers incented? Refine middle-management incentives to ensure that individuals are becoming certified and are adopting the change.	Must Have / Nice to Have
22	How do we measure that we are achieving our personnel development goals? Establish measurements to assess effectiveness and cover continuous improvement.	Must Have / Nice to Have
Training / Mentoring		
23	Do we have ongoing forums for employees to share best practices and learn from one other? Establish Communities of Practice (CoPs).	Must Have / Nice to Have
24	How do we pair certified and top performers with other employees to ensure consistency of techniques and adoption of change? Establish a mentoring program.	Must Have / Nice to Have
25	What training program is needed to support skills acquisition and career paths?	Must Have / Nice to Have
26	Who will deliver the training? Identify and secure training sources; put a delivery plan in place.	Must Have / Nice to Have

Figure 24. People quadrant future state analysis questionnaire.

#	Process Quadrant Future State Assessment	Priority
1	What will the process look like? Who will be doing it? What does the technology look like to support the process?	Must Have / Nice to Have
2	Where might the new process fall apart? How likely are each of these failures to occur? How big of a problem will be created at the failure points?	Must Have / Nice to Have
3	What mitigation strategies do we need in the new process? What will be the failure detection, resolution plan, and embedded contingency plan that is ready to go if the failure ever surfaces?	Must Have / Nice to Have
4	What will be the process to vet new ideas and to respond to continuous improvement suggestions?	Must Have / Nice to Have

Figure 25. Process quadrant future state analysis questionnaire.

#	Technology Quadrant Future State Assessment	Priority
1	What is the magnitude of technology needed to deliver services—from a small desktop application change to massive building of a new manufacturing plant? The scope of the planning and the amount of time it will take to make the change will be dependent on how big the technology effort is.	Must Have / Nice to Have
2	Will we be able to continue our current operations with the old technology until the new technology is ready?	Must Have / Nice to Have
3	What will the transition period look like? Will we shut down the plant for a week and send everybody on vacation while the changes are applied? Do we need to build an interim site that can keep the lights on temporarily and keep producing products and services? Do we need to stockpile inventory to handle customer orders during the outage?	Must Have / Nice to Have
4	Is the future state technology new to our organization? Do we already have the packaged software, tools, or a custom-built solution in-house?	Must Have / Nice to Have
5	Is the technology cutting edge for our industry?	Must Have / Nice to Have
6	Are we creating new technology?	Must Have / Nice to Have
7	What is the support plan for the future state technology?	Must Have / Nice to Have

Figure 26. Technology quadrant future state analysis questionnaire.

Recap of the Technique

To move the organization from here to there, you have to know where "there" is. Before you can plan the change, you must be able to describe the future state necessary to achieve the business vision. You also must identify which aspects of the change are "must have" and which are "nice to have."

An important part of the future world description includes everybody being on board and agreeing to the same vision. If you don't yet have buy-in from all of the impacted stakeholders, you're not ready to plan. Keep working to get consensus. The integrator should leverage the sponsor and the champions to gain agreement so that the change team can proceed with the next steps.

8 DECIDE ON ACHIEVABLE, RELEVANT CHANGE

Explanation of the Technique

For people to feel excited and engaged in making change happen, they have to believe that change is important and that it can be achieved. Is there a real case for change that is obvious—the "duh" factor? If the need for change is obvious, everybody understands why you're doing this. The improvement effort will have credibility.

There are many motivations for making a change. No matter how badly your organization needs to change, if there are no resources provided for the effort, it won't happen. Change takes time, planning, funding, and people.

To be realistic, the change has to have more than credibility. It also has to be achievable. Here are the questions to ask:

- Is there enough time to train and/or hire people to achieve the future competencies expected of the organization?

- Is there enough time to build, purchase, and install the future infrastructure, as well as train your people, before it is expected to be operational?

- Is there a clear metric defined so that the success of the change can be measured and proven?

- Are the metrics and new expectations reasonable and achievable?

Figure 27. People have to believe that the change is achievable.

Dreaming and planning big are good and can be very motivating. It's also important to be realistic about how much can be done. If the dream or plan is too big to be achieved, it's unbelievable. You'll have a hard time keeping people on board. We have seen sponsors become so enamored of lofty ideas that they fail because they don't take the time to assess whether the change can actually be delivered.

When you analyzed the future world, you decided on the criticality of each of the change aspects. It may happen that you come out of the future state analysis with a defined change that includes only critical needs and yet is still too big to tackle.

If it isn't possible to approach the change any other way, and the change is unrealistic, then really think long and hard about why the future vision is so hard to attain. Maybe it needs some adjustment.

Why Is This Step Important? What Happens if You Skip It?
To enable successful change to happen, your organization needs to acknowledge that this will not be free. Upfront expense needs to be incurred to implement the change. Even though the expense may be paid back many-fold after the organization is running differently, it's not realistic to think that you will be able to turn a key one day and have immediate benefit.

If you ever see that kind of a turnkey benefit, look a bit further back. We bet you'll find significant planning went into what appeared to be a seamless transition.

When you think about the resources required for the effort, consider how quickly the change needs to be instituted. The faster the pace, the more upfront money is needed. To make a rapid change, you will likely need to augment existing staff to still have business operations covered while the change is planned and managed.

If you are in a situation where you're trying to implement change but you have insufficient resources with no opportunity to get more—people, funding, hardware, software or physical workspaces—consider whether you can cut back the scope or pace of the change. Get it back to the point where it's manageable within what resources you have so you still have a chance at success. Getting to first base still helps you get closer to home plate.

Keep in mind what you identified as "must have" and what is "nice to have." This priority is going to be critical when you lay out your plan.

If the ideal future isn't achievable within the timeframe and the budget you have to work with, what is the minimum that you won't give up? If after identifying the minimum you still don't have the timeframe and budget, seriously reconsider what you have said is your minimum or whether this change should even be attempted. Be very clear on what is negotiable and what is not.

Checklist

Letter	SMART Goal Questions
S	Specific: Is the goal clear and unambiguous?
M	Measurable: How will we concretely measure progress?
A	Achievable: Do we know how the goal can be accomplished?
R	Relevant: Does this goal matter to our organization?
T	Time-bound: What is the target date when change is expected?

Figure 28. SMART questionnaire to test whether the change is relevant and achievable.

Recap of the Technique

Delivering successful change takes time, planning, funding, and people. For people to get on board, they need to believe that the change is meaningful and attainable.

Stretch goals may force employees to become creative and identify previously overlooked opportunities to improve your services, people, processes, and technology.

Be careful. Don't set an impossible expectation for the change team. When the impossible task fails, you will have lost all credibility and influence with the very people upon whom you will rely to actually make your organization better.

9 DEVELOP THE CHANGE MESSAGE

Explanation of the Technique

Once you understand your current world and have described your future world, you can fully define the scope of the wHolistic Change℠. The **change message** is a unifying vision statement that pulls together the success metrics with the quadrant impacts that will make the change a reality.

To create the change message, look at the differences between current and future state for the services, people, process, and technology impacts. For each of these aspects, identify what the change is, who is impacted (usually multiple stakeholders), and who is responsible for driving that component of the change. This gives you a detailed description of what needs to change.

Use the detailed differences you've identified for each aspect to create an overall change message. This is a brief statement that summarizes the case for change and the vision for the future. All levels of communication will include the change message. This ensures consistency of your messages and reinforces the fact that this change is needed and that it is taking place across the organization—not in a silo.

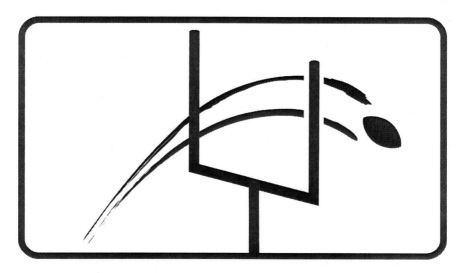

Figure 29. The change message: A unifying statement that summarizes the case for change and your vision for the future.

Why Is This Step Important? What Happens if You Skip It?
Having all of the changes delineated in one place helps you ensure that the communication plan and deployment plan do not have any gaps. It also helps ensure that the change team knows who is on point to make sure change happens.

In order to obtain resources—people, funding, hardware, software, and physical workspaces—to work on your change, the sponsor may require a scope statement detailing the business need for change and what degree of change will be implemented.

The change message gives:

- The sponsor a one-stop document describing the change scope to senior leadership and fellow champions.

- The change team manager a mechanism to ensure alignment of all change team members and impacted stakeholders to the change vision and who will deliver each aspect of the change.

- The communicator a unifying statement that will be used in all communications and training to ensure consistency of message.

A common "gotcha" is that not everybody has the same understanding of what the future world looks like. If there isn't a clear understanding, you might find that all of your stakeholders aren't working toward the identical goal and things can start to fall apart.

To make sure this doesn't happen, be really clear on defining the future. Key elements of this are:

- Defining the new processes.
- Defining the roles, responsibilities, and expectations for everybody who is involved in the future state services, people, processes, and technology.
- Getting your communication plan in place and executed.

Do employees know they will need training to provide the new services that will be asked of them? A prerequisite to people being successful is that they know what they need to do and are confident they can obtain the skills to do it.

Even though everybody may understand what the new process is, does she also understand that she is expected to go along with it? As opposed to thinking "this is (yet) another change initiative that is going to disappear in a few months so I'll just pretend to go along with it and everything will go back to normal soon."

Checklist
This change message includes sample language for an innovation culture change. Replace this text based on the change you define for your organization.

Overall Vision Statement
Large Brand Corporation recognizes the talent and commitment of our employees in delivering value to our customers every day. By establishing a culture of innovation, we will improve our products, processes, technology, and people. Large Brand Corporation's goal is to be the #1 employer of choice in our industry by 2016.

Services Change	Who is Impacted?	Who is Making Sure the Change Happens?
An Idea Generation Engine will be created and available to all employees to submit ideas for improvement. Ideas can be anything from new products or services for our customers to people, process, or technology changes that will improve how Large Brand Corporation does business (both internally and externally)	• All employees	• Innovation Change Team

People Change	Who is Impacted?	Who is Making Sure the Change Happens?
Training is needed to understand how to submit an idea to the Idea Generation Engine.	• All employees	• Innovation Change Team • Corporate Training
Communications are needed to understand the rationale for implementing a culture of innovation: Why it is important to Large Brand Corporation in terms of competitiveness and becoming an employer of choice	• All employees	• Executive Branch • Innovation Change Team • Corporate Communications • Human Resources

People Change	Who is Impacted?	Who is Making Sure the Change Happens?
Time will be set aside as part of employees' regular monthly job expectations to participate in innovation activities such as brainstorming, the Innovation Community of Practice and idea submission	• All managers • All employees	• Human Resources
Job promotion requirements will be updated to include constructive participation in innovation activities	• All employees	• Human Resources

Process Change	Who is Impacted?	Who is Making Sure the Change Happens?
A consistent, corporate-wide Idea Generation Engine process is being created to suggest an idea for improvement. Suggestions could be a new product or service, process improvement, technology, or people approach.	• All employees	• Innovation Change Team
There is a formal, monthly Innovation Community of Practice meeting to vet the submitted ideas and to decide whether to move forward with one or more ideas	• All employees • All department heads must name a designated representative	• Innovation Change Team

Process Change	Who is Impacted?	Who is Making Sure the Change Happens?
There is a formal, monthly Innovation Steering Committee meeting to review the vetted ideas and to decide sponsorship and funding to further research and/or implement the suggestions	• Executive members of the Innovation Steering Committee • All department heads potentially impacted, based on the suggested change	• Innovation Change Team

Technology Change	Who is Impacted?	Who is Making Sure the Change Happens?
A centralized Idea Generation Engine is being created to support the new innovation culture, including links to training materials, ability to suggest ideas, ability to view ideas submitted, and ability to view status of ideas in terms of vetting by the Innovation Community of Practice.	• Intranet Technology Team • All employees	• Intranet Technology Team • Innovation Change Team

Figure 30. Change message showing vision, change impacts, and who is responsible for making sure the change happens.

Decision Point: Proceed from Define to Plan?

The change message gives your sponsor a tool to communicate why the change is important and what the vision for the future is. The change message is a perfect way to decide whether you are ready to proceed into the planning phase.

The change message:

- Aligns the organization to a common future world.

- Is the basis to develop your deployment strategy.

- Acts as a foundation for a solid communication plan that will keep your organization informed as your change starts to take shape.

If your sponsor is not willing to share the change message and champion the change initiative, STOP NOW! Circle back to Chapter 4, "Obtain a Sponsor" and determine whether another executive sees the value and would be willing to sponsor your change to make it a reality.

Recap of the Technique
The change message will be used to drive all communications and to ensure alignment across all impacted stakeholders—internal and external.

For every aspect of the change, identify what the change is, who is impacted (usually multiple stakeholders), and who is responsible for driving that component of the change.

Create the one statement that summarizes the case for change and your vision for the future. All levels of communication will utilize the change message. This ensures consistency of information and reinforces the fact that this change is needed and is taking place across the entire organization.

10 TRAIN THE CHANGE TEAM

Explanation of the Technique

The wHolistic Change℠ approach is all about identifying the contributions that each player makes, while using their natural enthusiasm and sense of ownership to drive change. That statement just described a change agent. Change agents need to act as coaches and cheerleaders to guide your people through the steps they need to take to adopt the change.

Though other members of the change team do not have the same title as the change agents (that is, champion, change team manager, communicator, facilitator, integrator, owner, sponsor), they will still need the same skills in order to successfully act as agents of change within your organization:

1. Envisioning what is possible
2. Asking powerful questions
3. Listening actively
4. Welcoming ideas from others
5. Developing trusted relationships
6. Influencing without authority
7. Recognizing that the goal is change, not personal glory

Figure 31. Change agents: Coaches who guide the organization through adopting the change.

1. Envisioning what is possible

It will be critical that the people you identify to participate on the change team do not limit themselves to what exists today or to how the company "has always done things." The change team is required to think differently than how your company previously approached problems. The change team must challenge assumptions that will get people out of their comfort zones and therefore thinking about ways to tackle the business situation they now find themselves in.

Not all corporations have people who are professionally trained innovators. When you realize it is time for your company to change, you may need to call in outside expertise to guide your change team and, candidly, to get people truly thinking outside the box. This will ensure that you are creating a breadth of creative ideas for change.

What we especially love about brainstorming sessions is that they enable you to identify limits that you did not realize you had yet that don't need to limit you as you embark on your change. Brainstorming often brings to light areas where your team is going to need to focus to garner support from across all of your stakeholders. In addition, brainstorming will inform the plan you will develop.

For those of you who may get nervous about encouraging your people to think completely outside the realm of what you do today, take heart. Just because you facilitated an innovation session does not mean that you have to act on, implement, or adopt any or all of the ideas generated during the session. However, conducting a brainstorming session may create some of the most surprising and potentially lucrative ideas that your company otherwise might not have come up with.

Plus, this is a fabulous way to get your change agents energized about the fun and creative ways they will deliver change in your organization!

2. Asking powerful questions

A powerful question is an open-ended one. When subject matter experts and other employees provide feedback and express challenges with adopting the change, the change team needs to delve to make sure they truly understand the heart of the problem—not just the symptoms.

- Acceptable questions:
    - o Does everybody know her new role and the expectations of her?
    - o Could you delegate some of the change tasks to someone else?
- Powerful questions:
    - o Tell me about your challenges in the past with adopting a change and how you or your team handled them.
    - o Tell me about the people in your organization who are successful at adopting change.

3. Listening actively

The change team must demonstrate that they are interested in feedback from the subject matter experts and other employees. Active listening lets the organization know that the change team is seeking to truly understand others' perspectives.

The steps for active listening are:

1. Restate what you heard:
    - o Am I correct that the main challenge with the change is …?
2. Clarify:
    - o What is the biggest concern or issue that you feel we need to address immediately?

3. Show empathy:
   o It sounds like this has been a very frustrating experience. I know that change can be hard.

It is not the responsibility of the impacted employees to reach out to the change team and say why employees don't want to change. It is up to the change team to actively seek feedback and to consciously listen so you can hear what's really going on. This way you can determine what must happen in order for people to become willing to adopt the change.

4. Welcoming ideas from others
As part of a change team you will be presented with other people's ideas and opinions on how to do things "better."

You've already established your vision and you're running with it. It seems to be commonly understood and bought into. Why would you pause and consider making a change based on somebody's suggestion? Well, because it might actually be a great idea—and the right answer will be to say "yes!"

Take a breath, think it through, and see if you can incorporate the suggestion into what you're doing. If you adopt and integrate, you've just created another change agent who is going to be on your side and help you to drive the change.

If you conclude that the suggestion isn't beneficial and might harm what you're trying to accomplish, then it's time to stand your ground and say "No, thank you, but no."

Whenever you say no, there is a very real possibility of alienating the person who made the suggestion. It will be important to say no in such a way that she understands the perspective of the change team and that she comes to understand the vision. It may come to the point where she could be a champion or a change agent, even after you've just shot down her idea.

Sometimes people can't be persuaded and you may have to agree to disagree. Just be sure you've made an effort to understand their perspective.

5. Developing trusted relationships
The qualities that build trust—active listening, humility, being open to new ideas, respecting everybody's opinion—are also characteristics that the change team needs to foster. By encouraging the open, honest exchange of ideas while designing the transformational change for your organization, you will engender goodwill among the owners whose support you need to

actively implement the change at the ground level.

In fact, the people impacted by the change may come up with better ways to effect a change that is faster and more efficient than what the change team has designed. The only way to know if they have better ideas is to build professional, healthy relationships with the owners and subject matter experts across your organization.

6. Influencing without authority
Because the majority of the change team will be composed of middle management or front-line employees, they will need to be able to persuade people at or above their hierarchical level in the organization to give change a try. The change teams' titles will not convince anyone that they have to listen to these change agents. Therefore, the change team members will have to use other ways to encourage, cajole, and otherwise win over people who will already have their own priorities and goals.

In "Consulted References" at the end of the book, we list some books we use that can help the change team learn how to influence others. However, in order to really be able to practice and master the skills, work with your Human Resources department to identify a training class on influencing without authority or the art of persuasion and send the entire change team.

7. Recognizing that the goal is change, not personal glory
You will always need charismatic change agents who can persuade and engage people, as well as get them on board with the change. Change agents put their reputations on the line every time they advocate for the change and persuade their peers to pay attention and give it a try.

A change agent needs to be able to recognize the whole of the group. She needs to understand when her individual contribution to the change needs to slip into the background so that the group can drive the change forward. A leader is absolutely needed to get things off the ground and moving, yet once there is forward momentum, leading from behind is a crucial and effective strategy.

Especially when there is resistance to change, it will be critical for the change agents to be able to take a step back and recognize the value the change will bring to the organization. Feedback from even close friends might become negative when issues arise or unforeseen challenges cause a plan to have to be reworked.

Throughout it all, a change agent needs to have the self-awareness to be able to take a breath and realize that what matters is the goal, not personal glory.

Why Is This Step Important? What Happens if You Skip It?
Your change agents will be the front-line employees effecting change in your organization.

If you do not prepare them to act as change agents, here's what can happen:

#	Lack of Skill	Worst Case Scenario
1	Envisioning what is possible	Future state is limited to what constrains the organization today
2	Asking powerful questions	Change team reacts to symptoms, not the root cause
3	Listening actively	Mistrust of the change team and the change by owners, subject matter experts, and other impacted employees
4	Welcoming others' ideas	Owners, subject matter experts, and other impacted employees become alienated because they don't believe the change team understands the impact to their stakeholder
5	Developing trusted relationships	Future state is limited to what the members of the change team know about how the organization works
6	Influencing without authority	Change team is unable to persuade owners, subject matter experts, and other impacted employees to participate in the change
7	Recognizing that the goal is change, not personal glory	Isolation and distrust of everybody on the change team. People catch on to this quickly.

Figure 32. What happens if the change team is not trained appropriately?

If the change team is not trained to be change agents, the upshot is that the real business problem underlying your case for change will at best be barely achieved. At worst, it will not be achieved at all.

Your change will fail if you are not solving the root cause of your problem, if you cannot convince anyone in upstream or downstream business operations to participate in the change, or if you are not willing to recognize that you have to adapt your approach to your organization.

Checklist

#	Change Agent Skill Set	Training Content to Build Competency
1	Envisioning what is possible	• Brainstorming • Innovation • Creative team problem solving
2	Asking powerful questions	• Mentoring courses
3	Listening actively	• Facilitation skills • Mentoring courses
4	Welcoming others' ideas	• Improvisation • Creating positive team environments
5	Developing trusted relationships	• Building trust • Communication techniques • Cross-cultural or global training
6	Influencing without authority	• Influencing without authority • Art of persuasion • What motivates people
7	Recognizing that the goal is change, not personal glory	• Situational leadership • Emotional intelligence

Figure 33. Training content for the change team to develop change agent skill sets.

Work with your Human Resources department to identify the training classes available in your organization. If the classes are not offered by your corporate training department, Human Resources should be able to identify external trainers to perform onsite training, as needed.

Recap of the Technique
True behavioral change happens because people recognize the value of making the change and then purposely decide to act differently on an ongoing basis.

All members of the change team will need the appropriate expertise to fulfill their roles (such as project management or strategic thinking). More importantly, they will also need to master the soft skills to successfully act as agents of change within your organization in order to convince people outside their sphere of influence to change their behaviors:

1. Envisioning what is possible
2. Asking powerful questions
3. Listening actively
4. Welcoming others' ideas
5. Developing trusted relationships
6. Influencing without authority
7. Recognizing that the goal is change, not personal glory

The wHolistic Change℠ approach is all about identifying the contributions that each person makes to an organization and then using their natural enthusiasm and sense of ownership to drive change. Training the change team in these techniques will engender change agents across your organization. That is how change will gain momentum.

11 HANDLE RESISTANCE TO CHANGE

Explanation of the Technique

wHolistic Change℠ attempts to drive out fear by performing all of the tactical activities we have included in our approach. However, despite the best intentions, you will still encounter resistance to change.

These are the techniques we use to handle and overcome resistance to change:

1. Keep the change itself simple and easy to adopt.
2. Ensure that peoples' incentives are tied to the change.
3. Involve middle managers throughout the change planning process.
4. Recognize that resistance to change is normal.
5. Maintain your sense of humor.
6. Don't take anything personally.
7. Communicate constantly.

Figure 34. Resistance is natural: The goal is to drive out fear
so that people are willing to change.

1. Keep the change itself simple and easy to adopt

If the change is viewed as too onerous or as taking too long to see results, it will not be successful. People will give up before they truly give the change a chance.

Ensure that your case for change is clear and that you have built the support structure your organization needs. Depending on the nature of the change, the support structure may require templates, samples, job aids, and/or training materials to set your people up for successful adoption of the change. See Chapter 16, "Determine Training and Development Needs" for further information on ensuring that your employees have the tools they need to be able to change.

2. Ensure that people's incentives are tied to the change

If there is a disconnect between people's incentives and adopting the change, people will focus on how their bonuses are decided—even if they recognize that change is the right thing to do.

Engage Human Resources to align all impacted employee incentives to adopt the change:

- Front-line employee incentives are tied to adopting the change and to becoming certified, if applicable

- Middle-management incentives are tied to ensuring that individuals are embracing and adopting the change and that people are becoming certified, if applicable

- Owner incentives are tied to demonstrating commitment to embracing change and that their stakeholders are adopting the change

- Sponsor and/or champion incentives are tied to the business outcomes expected from the change

A key pitfall to delivering change is no or limited engagement of Human Resources in assessing the impact of the change to peoples' roles and responsibilities.

The role of Human Resources is to help hire and train workers to ensure the best results for your company. If Human Resources is not involved in the process, she may not understand the changes needed in employees in order to help incent the change. Or Human Resources may continue to hire people based on how the company previously did business, instead of how it needs to do business in the future.

3. Involve middle managers throughout the change planning process
Middle management will determine if behavior change will actually happen. They manage the front-line employees, set work priorities, and are ultimately responsible for the relationships with your customers.

Middle managers are also responsible for the training and development of their front-line employees. They are looked to as mentors when their employees have questions about how to handle a particular situation. If middle managers do not see the value of the change or if they view it as a nuisance and disruption to their business operations, the change will fail.

When roadblocks are thrown up by the middle managers, propose alternate ways to solve the issue. Try to get their input into an acceptable solution. When it's clear that they do not get to opt out and that their issue is being heard—and that you want their help solving the problem—middle managers are likely to cooperate and feel ownership of the solution.

In the event that a middle manager stubbornly refuses to participate in the change, engage her owner to determine the best way to handle the situation. Owners may be able to identify a trusted, credible, middle-manager peer who can persuade the resister to try the change. If that doesn't work, escalate to your sponsor for advice how best to handle the situation.

4. Recognize that resistance to change is normal

There will *always* be some form of resistance to change. When people are asked to think or behave differently from how they have become accustomed, there will naturally be some hesitation and fear.

People adapt to change at different rates and with varying degrees of ease. The people who are early adopters—your champions and change agents—will readily tell you how they feel. They have figured out why the change is important and they're going to give you ideas to keep going further. This group long ago moved beyond needing to be shown that change is possible.

For the people who are not early adopters, who are frightened of what is coming, or who don't believe that the expected result can be achieved; consider what their motivations might be for how they behave in a given situation. Ask where they are coming from and why you think they are acting the way they are.

Often, if we take the time to step back and ask what motivates the resister, instead of just reacting to how she is behaving, we are able to determine the best way to see the world through her eyes. Then we can come up with a strategy to get her to see our point of view or at least not become as frustrated when we don't see eye to eye.

5. Maintain your sense of humor

You are a change agent on the front line. You have poured your heart and soul into the vision of the future and have worked as hard as you possibly can to make it happen. A colleague has just told you that your ideas are "crazy, stupid, never going to happen, and they're going to ruin life as we know it."

It is critical for your sanity—and for that of the entire change team—to maintain perspective and to try to find the humor in the challenges you are facing. Is it likely that all of us and all of our executives are crazy and stupid at the same time? I know I already changed and am doing great, so is it possible that change can *never* happen? Will this change really ruin life as we know it?

Set aside time among the change team to regularly share your favorite quotes about resistance to change. Some of the things people say will provide great sources of humor. Remember that laughter is an excellent way to relieve stress as you drive change.

6. Don't take anything personally

This technique harks back to Chapter 10, "Train the Change Team." Recognize that the goal is change, not personal glory. Do not take resistance personally!

If you can manage it, disengage yourself from being the driver of the change. Try to step into a role of impartial observer, or perhaps, investigator. This is a great opportunity to ask a lot of "why" questions in order to understand the detractor's point of view.

There's a reason for her opposition. Knowing what it is can provide you with some valuable information:

- There may actually be a flaw in your plan and in what you're proposing for the future. Better to find that out as early as you can.

- The way she describes her opposition may give you a clue as to how you need to manage change for this person. Maybe the standard approach that seems to be working for everybody else isn't going to work for her.

- The person who has the opposition may be speaking only for herself or she might be expressing the opinions of a larger group who haven't yet said anything out loud.

- The person is worried about her future with the company. Fear is preventing her from being able to take action, any action, except for what she knows today.

- She just doesn't understand what she needs to do. This could signify a lack of clarity in the communications or inadequate training and development materials for employees to believe they can successfully change.

- The reason for her resistance truly is personal. Her opposition results from a sense of competition with you, or some similar motivation. This can make you aware of how you'll need to work with this person in the future. In this case, even though **it is** personal, don't take it personally. Do not let this derail you!

Good for you if you managed to step back from yourself and understand what the other person is telling you. With that knowledge, you can make a decision based on rational thought and not emotional reaction to being attacked. After understanding the reason for her opposition, you may rationally decide that where you're headed is just fine.

7. Communicate constantly

Before deciding to change, adults need to know the reason change is needed and how well change is taking hold. In order to control the perception of the change, you must provide constant communications— who, what, when, where, why, how, and how well. Lacking direct personal knowledge, people will make up their own stories.

If they don't hear directly from the change team, your employees will make up their own minds about whether the change is successful, whether your organization and customers are better off as a result of the change, or whether the change will continue to deploy or be cancelled. Rumor-generated change stories are often more negative than the truth and can engender resistance. Employees don't want to participate in anything that will make their jobs harder, dissatisfy customers, or waste their time.

Chapter 14, "Build the Communication Plan," discusses communication planning and controlling the messages in more depth. What is important to keep in mind is that people **will** discuss the change. If the change team doesn't tell them, someone else will.

Why Is This Step Important? What Happens if You Skip It?

Your change agents will be the first line of defense in dealing with resistance to change. Without the belief that they can successfully effect change in your organization, the change will not take hold.

Beyond knowing that change is important, change agents need to know that the frustrations and harsh comments they encounter will ultimately be worth the reputational risk they are taking by participating on the change team.

Here's how you can demonstrate that you value your change agents:

- Publicly **recognize** your change agents. Name them to the rest of the organization if they have a formal role as part of the change team. If they are not part of the formal change team, there are informal ways to recognize them. Give them credibility and tribute in your communications. Recognize their contributions to the success of the change.

- **Empower** your change agents to speak on behalf of the change team. Give them the knowledge and authority to provide updates to their peers, their owners, or even their stakeholders. Change agents can be the voice of change. The visibility of their role in the success of that change can be motivating for the change agents, as well as a great way to influence people who are still deciding whether they will change, too.

- Provide a **networking** opportunity for your change agents. Give them time to talk to one other and generate ideas or just to share resistance-to-change "war stories". This could be done through a formal or informal change agent Community of Practice (CoP).

- When change agents provide ideas, **take them seriously** and give them consideration. Where you can, incorporate the ideas into the change. This not only motivates the change agents to stay involved, it gives them credibility with their peers. You may also garner a few more change agents from the peer group.

If the leadership of the change effort that you're involved in doesn't understand the change agent role, describe it for them and try to persuade them to empower their change agents. Do it for no other reason than that it will make the leaders look good (and smart) when this group delivers the change for your organization.

Checklist

There are some changes that "stick" and some that don't. Change efforts that are successful and that manage to continue on, despite resistance to change, have some common characteristics.

#	Successful Change Characteristic	How You Know if Your Change Has This Characteristic
1	There is a clear message and everybody knows the reason the change is being made	Whether the message makes it through will be a result of the communication planning and execution. Without a clear message, confusion will reign after the change is underway and you won't have people working toward a common goal.
2	Life does not get harder as a result of the change	If the change has made daily life simpler and clearer, while people's jobs did not get harder or more complex, you've got something going that is sustainable.
3	The outcome of the change is valued and desirable	If the change makes you a better organization, what is not to like about it? Why would you not keep it going? If on a personal level your people also benefit from learning new skills or receiving new training, you have individual motivation for being on board.
4	The change is nimble and able to be continuously improved	When the change is too rigid and leaves no room for improvement, it can quickly become outdated. A nimble process that is adaptable to a changing business environment and marketplace leaves you positioned to be able to keep getting better.
5	Employee incentives are aligned with the change outcomes	There is no conflict between the expected change and how people's annual performance, bonuses, and promotions are decided.
6	There are constant communications about the change	There is a defined communication plan that is actively being executed. (See Chapter 14, "Build the Communication Plan.")
7	The change team is not burned out at the end of the project	The members of the change team want to play active roles on future change initiatives.

Figure 35. What is needed to make change "stick?"

Recap of the Technique

Here are the ways we successfully handle and overcome resistance to change:

1. Keep the change itself simple and easy to adopt.
2. Ensure that peoples' incentives are tied to the change.
3. Involve middle managers throughout the change planning process.
4. Recognize that resistance to change is normal.
5. Maintain your sense of humor.
6. Don't take anything personally.
7. Communicate constantly.

Since the change team will be composed of people with deep expertise in their specific roles (for example, change team manager or owner), they will need the ability to take a step back and determine whether they are over-engineering the change.

Based on the business need and the expected value that the change will bring, have you created a solution that someone from an impacted business operation will be able to pick up and effectively execute? If not, the resistance to change you are experiencing may be more than normal resistance; it may be a warning sign that your change cannot succeed as designed.

Maintain your perspective about what is truly important. Be willing to compromise in order to ultimately achieve your business goal.

12 DEVELOP THE DEPLOYMENT STRATEGY

Explanation of the Technique
Deployment planning falls within a standard project-planning paradigm. It isn't our objective here to tell you how to do project planning. Rather, our goal is to make sure that you've asked all of the right questions to enable you to determine a deployment strategy for your wHolistic Change℠ that is realistic and achievable.

1. To phase or not to phase?
2. What other changes are going on in the organization?
3. Can we pilot?

Figure 36. Before you deploy, you need a strategy.

1. To phase or not to phase?
Change can be deployed all at once ("big bang") or it can be phased in gradually. There may be some characteristics of what you're deploying that won't allow for the change to be phased in. Nevertheless, at least ask the questions in the Deployment Strategy Checklists to see if a phased approach might be an option.

In general, deploying in phases is less risky and allows for adjustments along the way, if needed.

2. What other changes are going on in the organization?
Another key aspect to consider when you are determining your deployment strategy is whether any other change activity is happening in your organization at the same time.

We have found that once a corporation decides to make a change, there tend to be multiple changes going on at the same time that involve the same stakeholders.

Your chances for success increase when you are aware of one another's goals, timelines, and key deliverables. This is also an opportunity to leverage one another's communication plans, since some of the same people will be impacted by the related changes.

We call mutually beneficial change initiatives "key alignments" because we will want to stay connected with and aligned to those efforts as our change moves forward.

There is a limit to the amount of change people or an organization can tolerate. It is better to be wildly successful with a few things than moderately successful with many.

3. Can we pilot?

Piloting the change is an approach that can be extremely useful in testing out the change as well as overcoming resistance to implementing the change.

In particular, if the approach to change is viewed as being too onerous or too full of components some owners consider to be "nice to haves," then conducting a successful pilot can give you the business metrics to engender champions who are willing to roll out your change more broadly across your organization.

Some criteria to consider when planning the pilot:

1. Define success. Make sure there is a clear definition upfront of what a "successful pilot" will look like.
    o What must be delivered to the customer?
    o What is the customer specification of quality of the product to be delivered?
2. Identify the project for the pilot. Ideally, use a project that has not succeeded in the past and for which you have metrics. This way you will be able to show the difference between the original approach and how people will behave differently due to the change.
    o Scope: The defined work to be achieved should be comparable between the baseline project or the old way of doing things and the pilot change project.
    o Schedule: How long did it take to deliver?
        ▪ Keep in mind that due to the learning curve, it may actually take longer for the pilot project to deliver than what the final timing will be once the change is operational.
        ▪ As the organization embraces the change and becomes more proficient at behaving differently, you can expect that it will take less time to deliver the same results and that the quality will continue to improve.
    o Budget: How much did each project cost?

- o People: How many individuals did it take to deliver the scope of the project? What were their skill sets?
- o Achievement of customer satisfaction: How well did each project deliver to market?

3. Name the people who will participate in the pilot.
   - o Ideally, the pilot participants should be the change agents you have identified across your organization. Having people who recognize the need to change and who are willing to try something new will also mean that the pilot participants will be willing to roll with challenges as they encounter issues.
   - o During the course of the project, these individuals will be great sources of feedback to propose products or services; process and procedure; technology; and training and development needs as you think about rolling the change out more broadly.

4. Report progress: Who needs to know about the pilot and how frequently?
   - o The communicator will need to keep everybody apprised of the progress of the pilot(s).
   - o Make sure to celebrate the successes along the way.

Depending on the breadth of your change, you may want to do more than one pilot to demonstrate that your results are not a fluke and that your change is something that will work on multiple types of initiatives.

If you choose to conduct multiple pilots simultaneously, make sure your change team has the bandwidth to mentor all of the projects through the learning curve. Otherwise, stage the timing of the pilots so that the change team can support them successfully.

Why Is This Step Important? What Happens if You Skip It?
The purpose of project management is to deliver business outcomes. Your organization has decided that it is time to change and it has a solid case for making the change. Now it is up to the change team manager to coordinate across all of the impacted stakeholders. She must determine the best way to plan all of the activities and their interdependencies, as well as to deliver the results.

As we stated in Chapter 1, "Assemble the Change Team," it is the responsibility of the change team manager to make sure that:

- There is a plan.

- Everything is going according to plan.

- Everything gets back on plan when there has been a bump in the road.

The change team manager is responsible for:

- Managing the risks, issues, dependencies, and constraints.

- Making sure that all of the other change team members are doing their jobs.

- Ensuring that progress is being made toward the change goal.

Lack of thoughtful project planning causes frustration, rework, and, potentially, the inability to deliver on business commitments.

Checklist

#	Services Quadrant Deployment Questions
1	What are the new products or services that we are going to ask our organization to provide?
2	When can we be prepared to provide those new products or services? What are the steps that must happen in order to be ready, such as training, new hiring, marketing, and Human Resources aligned?
3	How quickly do we need to be able to collect metrics to prove out the value from the change? Larger deployments over periods of time will take longer to provide metrics.
4	If the phased rollout of the change will be planned and executed jointly with any other mutually beneficial change initiatives (key alignments) that are ready to deploy at the same time, will we wait for them? Or ask them to wait for us?
5	Are there key customer or market commitments that cannot be affected by the change? If there are specific high-profile deliverables that cannot afford to be missed, leadership may want to consider the timing of the change rollout and the timing for the specific people involved in those projects to adopt the change.

Figure 37. Services quadrant deployment strategy questionnaire.

#	People Quadrant Deployment Questions
1	How much of the future state operational support materials must be in place prior to deployment, such as templates, samples, job aids, career paths identified, and incentives tied to the change? Can some future state materials be developed concurrently during a phased rollout?
2	Is there a specific stakeholder who is more likely to be successful with change, perhaps based on past experience or the characteristics of the people who are in the business unit?
3	Are we planning to deploy to a complete organizational entity? This will mean providing the depth of training and mentoring to one business unit.
4	Who are interested and willing to be early adopters? • Can we leverage stakeholders who want to change first? • Are there specific individuals who could become certified mentors of the change for their business units?
5	Are there specific interdependencies between departments that would rule out one or more business units from participating in a pilot? Or would it mean the departments have to deploy in the same phase?
6	How many organizational units does the change team have the capacity to support at one time during deployment?
7	What mechanism(s) will be used to train people? • Will training be provided by internal or external training organizations? What is their availability to schedule training? • How will training be scheduled and coordinated for people in geographically diverse locations? • How scalable is the training? Does deployment need to be constrained based on training capacity? • How quickly after training will people be expected to adopt the change? Be aware that it is best if the training is delivered "just in time."

Figure 38. People quadrant deployment strategy questionnaire.

#	**Process Quadrant Deployment Questions**
1	Does the entire process change? Or will we change only one activity, or a subset of activities, within a process?
2	Can the process be isolated to do a controlled or phased change?
3	What returns the most value? What are the activities in the process that can provide the most benefit by being improved? Do we want to deploy those first?
4	What are the characteristics of the process? Is the process complex enough to prove out the value of the change, yet not so complex that the results of the change are obscured and the process is very hard to implement? For example, if it takes building a new factory, this is an expensive way to prove a point about your process.
5	Who and how will the change be governed to ensure quality of output and achievement of success metrics? Ability to scale governance may affect the deployment strategy.
6	Who and how will the change team respond to continuous improvement suggestions? How will the change team receive and vet feedback? Make changes to services, people, process, and/or technology? Communicate outcome? Ability to scale continuous improvement may affect the deployment strategy.

Figure 39. Process quadrant deployment strategy questionnaire.

#	Technology Quadrant Deployment Questions
1	Does the change require new infrastructure to be in place? Does it need to be a turnkey operation? ("Turnkey" refers to a complete cutover of everything at a specified time.)
2	If the change is not a turnkey deployment, how long will the old technology still be around to support a gradual move to the new?
3	Will this be piloted or is it a wholesale change? Can it be piloted with a small, simple, controlled environment but still be large enough to capture meaningful results and feedback?
4	Do we need to purchase hardware, software, or tools available in the market?
5	How much configuration will be needed to make the technology support our services?
6	If we are creating new technology, what is the lead time for research and development, design, testing, and implementation?
7	What are the support and maintenance plans for the technology?
8	If we pilot, will production fixes be applied to pilot environments? Who will decide which fixes are applied?

Figure 40. Technology quadrant deployment strategy questionnaire.

Recap of the Technique

The deployment strategy asks how and how quickly you will implement change throughout your organization.

When all questions have been answered about the services, people, process, and technology deployment considerations, you should have enough information to make an informed decision about the best way to plan your change rollout.

13 CREATE THE CHANGE ROAD MAP

Explanation of the Technique

wHolistic Change℠ advocates creating a visual representation of your effort that's called a **change road map**. We do this using the quadrant construct of services, people, process, and technology.

On the road map, lay out the milestones for when you plan to have the pieces of the change in place. Now think about all of the interdependencies, and lay those milestones out on the road map. Position them to show what needs to be ready before, after, or simultaneously.

When the sequence of the milestones on the change road map doesn't match with the actual change plan, then you'll need to adjust the change plan or strategy. For example, your people need training in the new technology before the go-live date; however, the change plan shows that the technology isn't delivered until the go-live date. You'll either need to change the go-live date to allow time for training or you'll need to figure out some other way to get your people trained.

The change road map is an excellent communication device to drive common understanding and sense of commitment for what is about to happen. Include not only your change but also show key milestones of any other changes planned that are impacting your stakeholders' services, people, processes, and technology. This way, you can quickly determine if you are about to overload—and possibly overwhelm—your people.

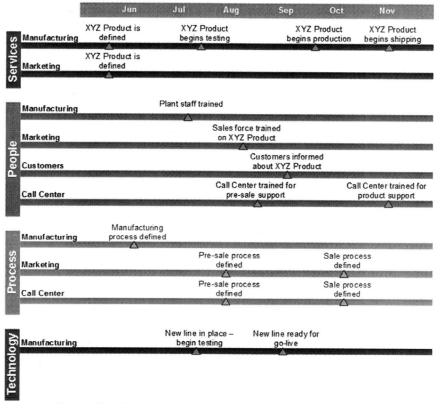

Figure 41. The change road map: Show the milestones and quadrant impacts.

Make sure that the road map includes the end customer as a stakeholder. Lay out impacts and communicate to your customers with enough advance notice so that they can do what needs to be done on their end to accommodate the new or changed service or product.

Why Is This Step Important? What Happens if You Skip It?
Another benefit of the change road map is to identify where there might be synergies. For example, if your department is rolling out a new tool that can also be a solution for another department, there might be ways to coordinate your deployment dates and communications.

If you demonstrate thoughtfulness in terms of how much change you expect your people to master in a given period of time, it will foster more willingness on behalf of impacted employees to become change agents.

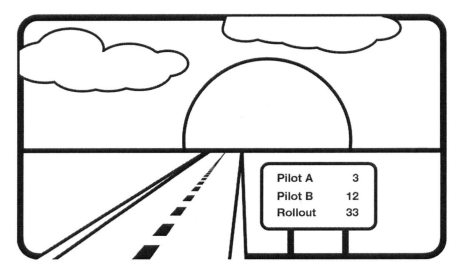

Figure 42. The change road map depicts milestones along the way.

Based on all of the changes affecting your stakeholders, you should take the time to identify and thoughtfully plan. If you don't, it often results in one or more of the following:

- **Anger** directed at the change teams. Don't you people talk to each other?

- Silent **entrenchment**. Impacted employees recognize that they just can't possibly change everything at once and therefore sit out and wait for senior leadership to tell them what to do. Or they wait for the initiative to go away.

- **Escalation** to senior leadership. Middle managers go to their owners or executive leadership and ask for a decision regarding what takes top priority

- Change **burnout**. Employees who try to do it all get frustrated and ultimately lose faith that change is possible. Their performance degrades over time due to stress and conflicting or competing priorities.

- Loss of **top talent**. In the end, top performers decide that the expectations of your organization are not worth it and they find new jobs, often with your competitors.

Keep in mind that once you develop the change road map and gain a better understanding of all the changes simultaneously impacting your stakeholders, you may need to revisit your deployment plan.

Checklist
wHolistic Change^{SM} approaches change from a perspective of "what" (services) are being done by "whom" (people); "when," "where," and "why" (process); along with any tools or infrastructure (technology) that are needed.

All of these aspects need to be coordinated in your deployment plan so that the interdependencies are in place and ready to go at the right time.

#	Change Road Map Development
1	Lay out the milestones for when each piece of the change is planned to be in place: • Services • People • Process • Technology
2	Think about all of the interdependencies and lay those milestones on the road map. Position them to show what needs to be ready before, after, or simultaneously. Examples: • Have people been informed about and prepared for the change? • Have we trained people in time to adopt the change? • Will technology be in place to be able to conduct the training? • Have we revised the career paths and/or development standards based on the change? • Have job descriptions and compensation rates been adjusted for market rates?
3	Have we included the key milestones from other change efforts that are impacting our stakeholders? • If the phased rollout of the change will be planned and executed jointly with any other change initiatives that are ready to deploy at the same time, will we wait for them? Or ask them to wait for us? • What happens if the other change initiatives miss their milestones? Will we deploy anyway? Or will we delay and wait for them?

Figure 43. Change road map checklist.

Recap of the Technique

The change road map is a visual tool to communicate the change implementation plan and to double-check that everything is coordinated. By using this technique, you can demonstrate to your organization that you've done everything necessary to make sure that all aspects of the change are ready at the right time and that you haven't overloaded any particular stakeholder.

14 BUILD THE COMMUNICATION PLAN

Explanation of the Technique

Communication planning requires an understanding of the organization, the change, and the key messages that are most important for the organization to understand. What your audience cares about and how you market the change to them will determine how quickly and how successfully the wHolistic Change℠ will take hold.

Like deployment planning, it isn't our objective here to tell you how to do communication planning. Rather, our goal is to make sure that you've asked all of the right questions to enable you to determine a communication plan that is relevant and inclusive of everybody who needs to know about the change.

As we mentioned in Chapter 1, "Assemble the Change Team," your communicator will make sure that everybody impacted is informed and understands what her new world is going to look like.

If possible, this person should come from a marketing or communications background. She will have a clear understanding of all the communication tools available and can recommend the most effective ways to communicate with everybody impacted by the change (internal and external). In addition, she will know how to brand the messages so people start to recognize the change as they see it reinforced through multiple avenues.

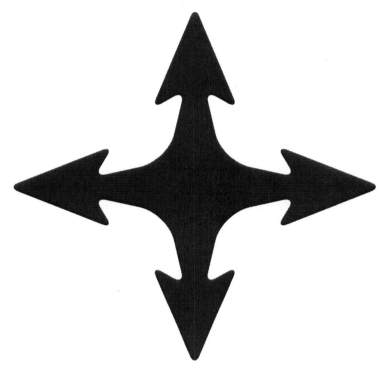

Figure 44. Communications must be multidirectional to tell everybody what is going on.

Key components to develop the communication plan:

1. Identify the target audience for messages and what they care about.
2. Brand the change.
3. Determine the frequency and format of communications, by audience.
4. Consider the culture.

1. Identify the target audience for messages and what they care about
Depending on where a person sits within your organization, she will have different concerns about the change and how it impacts her:

- What changed front-line employee behavior will look like in terms of services offered, processes used, employee attitudes expressed, technology used, and customer satisfaction response

- How the change will be measured to demonstrate that change is happening
- How to manage the impacted employees through the change:
  - If middle-level managers do not have experience mentoring people through change, they may require training. Middle-level managers will need to help their employees through the grieving process for the old way of doing things and toward the new vision for the company.
  - If the sponsor and champions do not have experience mentoring an organization through change, they may require training. Sponsors and champions will need to help the organization as a whole through the grieving process for the old way of doing things and toward the new vision for the company.
- What changed organizational behavior will look like in terms of services offered, process adoption, modified employee attitudes, technology effectively used, and customer satisfaction.

Here are some of the reasons for the different directions of communication flow that are needed in your communication plan:

Top-down communication (from your sponsor and champions):
  - Sharing the vision (change message)
  - Sharing the plan for reaching the vision (change message)
  - Making sure everybody knows about the impact to her daily life
  - Persuading everybody of the value of the change to minimize resistance
  - Aligning on a common goal
  - Celebrating successes
  - Acknowledging failures
  - Communicating risks and issues
  - Communicating status and progress
  - Asking for support and involvement

Lateral or sideways communication (from all change team members to their peers):
- o Discovery and idea generation
- o Consensus building
- o Brainstorming and problem solving
- o Solution sharing

Bottom-up communication (from impacted stakeholders to the change team):
- o Making needs known
- o Making suggestions for improvements
- o Raising risks that have actually become issues and asking for resolution
- o Sharing successes
- o Sharing failures

2. Brand the change

Leverage the communicator's skills to create a brand for your change. A logo and a color scheme for all change-related communications will help people start to recognize the change message as they see it reinforced through multiple mechanisms over time. Branding will uniquely distinguish your particular change, while also helping to ensure that perception of the change is consistent and positive.

3. Determine frequency and format of communications, by audience

When you start planning how you are going to communicate about your change effort, keep in mind what it will take for each of the impacted people to understand both the big picture and the details that are pertinent to them.

- Your big-picture message needs to get everybody aligned with what the change is all about and to help everybody understand why the change is happening:
  - o This level is all about vision and the future world picture.
  - o This level needs to get people excited about what's coming and align them with the vision, or at least reassure them enough to allay their fear.

- Once you've communicated the big picture, circle back with another level of communication that gives the details to the impacted people. This level will give as much information and answer as many questions as possible:

- o Not everything may be figured out yet. Even so, *anything* you can factually tell people is better than nothing. In the absence of information, people will make up their own facts.
- o Acknowledge everything you can't yet tell them and let them know when they can expect to hear more.
- o Try to tie the details back to the high-level points that were made. This lets people know how their individual contributions fit into the big picture and it can help them feel ownership in helping your organization achieve its goal.

You will most likely need to iterate through the levels of communication more than once as your change effort is in progress. Go back to the higher level of communication if either of the following happens:

- You can see that people have lost the understanding of what you're trying to accomplish.

- Your change has morphed into a different initiative and you need to drive a new understanding.

People learn in different ways. The communicator will need to determine the most effective ways to communicate with everybody impacted by the change so that people start to recognize the change as they see it reinforced through multiple avenues.

Often, the communicator will have access to mass mailer tools to which the change team might not. This individual is usually also plugged in to the corporate calendars of events, so she will be able to help the change team create the appropriate timing to address all communication needs and mechanisms:

- Emails and newsletters
- Corporate intranet articles
- Webinars
- Lunch N Learns
- Instructor-led training
- Web-based training
- Departmental quarterly or annual meetings.

4. Consider the culture

Before you finalize your communication plan, consider how your culture impacts stakeholder action or inaction:

- Does your organization pay attention to the written word? Or is it more verbal?

- Is there a particular communication method that your organization pays more attention to than another?

- Will somebody only pay attention to something if it comes directly from her management as opposed to from a central source?

To get your message heard and to keep people informed about ongoing change, consider your culture.

Based on what works best for your organization, identify communication channels (top-down, lateral, and bottom-up), create new communication channels if you need them, and then execute your plan.

Why Is This Step Important? What Happens if You Skip It?

Bottom line, how effectively you communicate can enable your change to happen smoothly or it can make it fail miserably.

We have seen changes fail where communication is done through limited communications to a small audience. Additional people that are also impacted by the change are not included in the distribution, so they don't know that the process has changed. The impacted individuals find out months later when they go to perform an activity that they do perhaps monthly or quarterly and are informed they have done it "wrong."

The result is business delay while the impacted people try to decipher what changed and to navigate the organizational labyrinth to find out how to make the new process work. In one worst-case scenario, an owner was relieved of his duties in owning a particular process because of the negative business impact his poor change approach caused.

To avoid the worst-case scenario, ask yourself:

- Has the communication plan covered everybody who has to know about the change so that there won't be any hidden obstacles that appear later?

- Have the communications done the job of informing, persuading, and motivating?

One last key element of communication is critical. Communication goes two ways. It's not only important that you send information out. Be open and willing to hear what's coming back. Be prepared to take action on what you hear.

Checklist

The degree of impact of the change may require a different degree of communication in terms of the impact to the services, people, processes, and technology.

#	Communication Plan Development
1	Awareness: Ensure that absolutely everybody impacted by the change is aware of what is happening, why, when, what it means for her, and how she can get involved and/or learn more. Example: • Develop a branded, quarterly newsletter to send to a broad distribution, including all executives, owners, the change team, and everybody even remotely affected by the change. This distribution list will grow over time as more people become aware of the change; therefore, every edition should: • Share the vision • Celebrate successes • Address issues that have arisen • Communicate status and progress • Explain how to get more information

#	Communication Plan Development
2	Understanding: Ensure that the people whose roles are affected by the change understand what it means to them. Recognize that people learn through a variety of mechanisms. Develop your communication plan to support multiple media: • Some people are more comfortable reading written materials. • Some prefer a hands-on approach using a case study. • Some like attending a seminar where someone explains the materials. • Some like tests that reinforce what they have learned. Partner with your company's training department to develop the best materials based on your specific target demographic to ensure that the materials created achieve the learning objective: • Employees truly understand how their jobs and approaches need to change. • Employees know what tools are available to help them successfully make the change. Beyond the initial training to achieve understanding, keep people informed as the change continues to evolve: • As lessons are learned and continuous improvement feedback is incorporated, the people who need to understand the change will have to be kept up to date on the evolution of the change. • By keeping them informed, they can support the change as adoption extends throughout the organization. • In addition, if these people are resisters to change, seeing increased momentum and examples of true successes may overcome their reluctance to adopt the change.

#	Communication Plan Development
3	Adoption: Ensure that the people whose services, roles, processes, and technology are directly affected by the change behave differently. Develop a practitioner Community of Practice (see Chapter 15, "Establish a Change That Lasts"), to provide a closed loop feedback mechanism to the change team about the following: • What is working • What is not working • What is missing to truly achieve critical mass in terms of adoption Beyond the initial training to achieve understanding and then adoption, keep people informed as the change continues to evolve: • As lessons are learned and continuous improvement feedback is incorporated, the people who deliver the change will have to be kept up to date on the evolution of the change so they can do their jobs and provide the best possible service to your customers. • By keeping them informed, the adopters can continue to act as change agents and champions as adoption extends throughout the organization.

#	Communication Plan Development
4	Mentoring: Identify specific employees to achieve a level of competence in the change such that these individuals can act as coaches or trainers to others within the organization. The good news is that, at the beginning, these people will be forgiving that the templates, examples, and end-to-end coordination of all of the changes will not be defined:
	• They will help create the templates, tools, examples, training, and process flows showing how the change is being incorporated into how you do business.
	• The change team will then communicate the developed materials as demonstration that the organization is dedicated to making the change a reality (through communication mechanisms 1–3).
	As the change becomes operational, continue to keep these people informed of the change evolution so they mentor others consistently based on how the change is truly taking shape. Create a mentor Community of Practice that focuses on:
	• Updating the certified employees on any new developments in terms of services, people, process, and technology
	• Giving them a direct link to all of the templates, tools, examples, and training materials that are kept current by the change team
	• Keeping the mentors informed, so they can continue to act as change agents and **you will** ensure consistency of adoption as it extends throughout the organization.

Figure 45. Communication plan checklist: The greater the change impact, the more communications are needed.

Recap of the Technique

Communication planning requires an understanding of the organization, the change, and the key messages that are most important for the organization to understand. Everybody impacted by the change needs to be informed and understand what her new world is going to look like.

Based on the communication tools available in your organization, leverage the communicator to determine the most effective ways to communicate with everybody impacted by the change and to brand the messages so that people start to recognize the change as they see it reinforced through multiple avenues.

Key components to develop the communication plan:

1. Identify the target audience for messages. Tailor messages based on what they care about as well as on what the change means to their services, people, processes, and technology.
2. Brand the change for consistency and recognition over time.
3. Determine the frequency and format of communications, by audience.
4. Consider the culture and its impact on stakeholder action or inaction.

15 ESTABLISH A CHANGE THAT LASTS

Explanation of the Technique
Different changes require different degrees of operational support in order to sustain them. Nevertheless, all change management plans must include a continuous improvement feedback loop to give your organization the means to provide feedback on how well the wHolistic Change℠ is taking hold and suggestions for how to make it better.

As you're setting up your continuous improvement structure, you need to understand the culture because that will influence how people will provide suggestions for improvement.

If your organization's culture is open and everybody's thoughts are welcomed, then make your continuous improvement suggestions public and include an element of personal recognition and identification for the submitter.

If the culture is a bit more cautious, then set up your continuous improvement process and structure to allow for a suggestion to be submitted privately. Include an opportunity to make it public after it has been vetted and allowed to move forward. At that point, it may be safe to acknowledge the submitter.

Your organizational culture impacts continuous improvement in the same way that it impacted your communication plan. You'll need to consider the culture when you decide on the right communication vehicles and methods to keep people informed about the continuous improvement changes.

Figure 46. Continuous improvement is a closed loop: Keep people
informed and listen to feedback.

It may make sense to develop multiple Communities of Practice for
continuous improvement. Depending on the type and degree of change, the
needs and concerns may vary per community:

- Practitioners will be expected to behave differently once the change
  is implemented.

- Middle managers will be expected to manage their people differently.

- Stakeholders will have owners who are indirectly affected by the
  change.

- Owners and change agents will be expected to maintain the change
  and teach future employees, once the change team is disbanded.

One way to get the group started may be to form a "forum" of people with
a common interest. Task them with reviewing and refining the change that
is being proposed. From their perspective as the impacted group, they'll

have an opportunity to weigh in with their thoughts, listen to everybody else's thoughts, and feed off of each other's ideas. In the end, they will create something that is part of all of them and they will all have a vested interest in making it work.

This may be asking people to step outside of their comfort zone, because they'll need to be willing to speak up with their opinions and to negotiate with their peers.

Have somebody facilitate the forum at the beginning in order to help the group develop their skills, prepare the group for owning its Community of Practice, and keep it moving forward after the facilitator is no longer needed.

Why Is This Step Important? What Happens if You Skip It?

The continuous improvement feedback loop from and to the change team is critical. This ensures that the change team stays in touch with the people directly affected by the change while they are going through the change, identifies issues and risks early on, and keeps the key stakeholders informed throughout the deployment as adjustments need to be made.

Communities of Practice are wHolistic Change's℠ preferred way to get direct feedback from your stakeholders. CoPs build credibility for the change team with the people affected by the change because the communities demonstrate that the change team understands the human impact of the change and that they want to involve the employees in formulating the change.

The questions to be answered are:

- What happens once a continuous improvement suggestion is submitted?
- Who decides what happens to it?
- Does it go up the chain of command? Does it go to a committee of peers? Or does it go through some other process?

It's critical to have a level playing field to make sure that people are comfortable opening up and presenting their ideas. If you can set up the feedback loop in a manner that allows people to feel confident that nobody else gets to just squash their idea—and that management can't negatively react to any idea—you'll find people contributing.

If you can also set up the feedback loop so that everybody can see the other ideas that have been generated and allow her to add on to those ideas, you will have a great process in place to really support creativity.

One characteristic of unsuccessful changes is having no clear organizational understanding of the continuous improvement process. Nor is there an understanding of how or when feedback will be implemented if the change is not working.

A closed feedback loop is especially important if the change team does not understand the ripple effect of the change they are implementing. The impacted stakeholders need a mechanism to explain the impact and to participate in redesigning the change to ensure business continuity and to ensure no disruption to your customers.

There is a reason for making sure that your employees are involved and that you've established a communication channel where they can provide feedback. If employees are shut out of the change process, what they have to say will still be said. However, you, as an organization, will miss out on hearing it. Or else you will hear it during exit interviews as top performers, and, potentially, customers leave.

Checklist

Being ready for continuous improvement means that you've defined your feedback loop, the roles and responsibilities, and how it will function.

#	Continuous Improvement Process Questions
1	How will employees provide continuous improvement feedback on the change, for those employees eager to give feedback?
2	How will the change team generate continuous improvement suggestions based on experience with the change? For the people who are reluctant to speak up, how will the change team encourage feedback?
3	Who will monitor the continuous improvement process for feedback?
4	Who will govern and ultimately make the decision if a change is needed to the services, people, process, and/or technology solutions?
5	How often will updates be made? Monthly? Quarterly?
6	Who will implement the change(s) to the services, people, process, and/or technology solutions?
7	What will happen if there is an emergency break or fix needed?
8	What will happen if a feedback change is denied? Who will communicate the denial and reasoning?
9	How will we verify that the training is occurring to ensure that feedback is coming from people who have been trained and that training is sufficient?
10	How will we verify that the new processes are being followed to ensure that feedback is coming from people using the process and that the process works?
11	How will we measure the depth and breadth of deployment of the change to ensure that the change is taking hold and that there are no gaps?
12	How will we measure quality of adoption to ensure that people are applying the change well and to identify if more or different training is needed?
13	How will any updates be communicated to the practitioners?
14	How will we keep the key alignment change initiatives involved in and informed of our continuous improvement process and changes?

Figure 47. Continuous improvement process checklist.

Recap of the Technique

Having a mechanism to provide continuous improvement feedback on the change makes people feel valued and more likely to be willing to try something new. Creating Communities of Practice of employees impacted by your change is a great way to give a voice to the people impacted by the change.

By participating in a CoP, community members exchange ideas, collaborate, and learn from one another. Members identify best practices, develop expertise, and are able to access a constant flow of information to do their jobs better and more consistently.

16 DETERMINE TRAINING AND DEVELOPMENT NEEDS

Explanation of the Technique

The goal of wHolistic Change℠ is to ensure that people are successful at getting through the change and continue to maintain the new world on an ongoing basis. Training and development, either formal or informal, are likely to be needed for your people to achieve competency in the skills they will need.

Determine if training is something that the organization will pay for or if the employee will be asked to contribute. For example, if you need people to be certified in a particular skill and if that skill is very portable, then achieving that certification can be as valuable to the employee as to the organization. In this case, it may be reasonable to ask for the employee to do the training on her own time and to even pay for it herself.

Take a look at how other organizations have approached providing training for their employees in similar situations. Then decide if you will stay within the norm or if you might do more as a way to differentiate your organization as an employer of choice.

Figure 48. Training and development: Give your employees
the tools they need.

One question to ask when designing the training and development materials: Does your employee base have the fundamental training (either hard or soft skills) to be able to leverage the materials you are creating to take them to the next level?

If not, then we suggest you work with your Human Resources and training departments to identify best-in-breed classes—perhaps industry courses—to supplement the deployment plan you develop.

The key is to focus on setting your employees up for success and show them you are committed to giving them all the tools they need to adopt the change. This way, you will create an environment that incents your staff to take the leap and help make the change a reality.

Why Is This Step Important? What Happens if You Skip It?
The business of change is hard. The people who are impacted by the change are the ones who pay the toll.

One characteristic of changes that fail is offering no or limited training to ensure that the change is consistently applied. Often, people require some form of support to modify their behavior. If the change involves a process redesign and if people are not given the proper training to implement the change on a day-to-day basis, then the change will not happen. Instead, individuals will find a workaround to do the bare minimum to appear to comply.

Recognize what it is that is changing about your employees' lives and the nature of the stress and instability that will cause.

Often, the change could be perceived as negative because:
- Their job is being eliminated.
- They are being asked to do different work that they are not as interested in.
- Their job is getting harder because they will now have to do more with less.

The change could also be perceived as positive and still could cause stress of a different nature because:

- New responsibility can cause the fear of failure at the same time as excitement to tackle something new.
- Increased visibility can cause nervousness whether they can rise to the challenge along with the thrill of being able to prove they can do it.

With recognition of the root cause of the stress, you can strategize on how best to reduce and relieve the stress from the root cause. Allow somebody to take an objective look around her and understand that it's really going to be OK.

When people are being displaced, help to relieve their stress and anxiety by putting in place a transition team that will be responsible for helping people to find a new position either within or outside of the company. This could be considered a "nice to have," but if your organization does a good job of helping displaced workers, it will indicate to the workforce that you treat your people well. Even though you may be reducing headcount right now, when you are hiring again, they'll be interested.

When people will be taking on new responsibilities and challenges, help to relieve their stress and anxiety by making sure they have received all of the training they need. Assign them a mentor to help them with their career development, that is, somebody who knows the ins and outs of the organization and who can help them to be successful in their new role.

Checklist

Work with Human Resources and the Communities of Practice to identify the training and development materials necessary to drive and support your change. Remember, each Community of Practice is composed of the people who know how the organization actually works today: your employees.

#	Training and Development Needs
1	Reaction to the change: Potentially, all of the people in your organization will need to be aware that the change is happening and why it is happening. Ask yourself: • Beyond the communications about the change message, how will you ensure that everybody has been made aware of the change? • How favorably will all levels of the organization react to the change? This will affect the degree and rate of adoption.
2	Increase in knowledge about the change: A subset of the people in your organization will need to really understand the change. Build upon the first step by starting to delve deeper into how the change will affect what they do on a day-to-day level: • What services will change? • What roles and responsibilities will change? • What processes will change? • What technology will change? • What training will be needed? • How will people be set up for success?
3	Application of the change in terms of behavior change: Once the knowledge of the change is absorbed, people will be expected to actually apply the change in their day-to-day jobs. Ensure that behavior changes by creating: • Templates • Job aids • Examples • Standard operating procedures • Mentoring support for current staff • Training and mentoring for new hires

#	Training and Development Needs
4	Measurement of effect of the change on the business: At the beginning of the process, your organization defined what successful change would look like and made a case for the change in terms of business value. Close the loop by ensuring that: • There is an effective way to actually verify that the change is happening. • The measurement process is closely tied to communications in order to encourage the change to continue until it has fully taken hold. • The measurement process is also closely tied to the continuous improvement process to identify if and why behavior change is not happening as expected. Adjust training levels 1–3, as needed.

Figure 49. Training and development needs checklist.

Decision Point: Proceed from Plan into Execute?
Once your training and development needs are determined, you have finished change planning. This is an important time to check in with your sponsor and determine whether the case for change success metrics justify the scope, schedule, budget, and people it is going to take to make your change a reality.

If your sponsor believes the plan does not merit the expected business benefit, stop and have a discussion. Now that you understand the magnitude of the change, ask yourself:

- Have you uncovered some unforeseen benefits along the way?

- Have you identified some mutually beneficial change initiatives that will enable you to achieve economies of scale by deploying together?

- Have you uncovered important information why previous change initiatives have failed?

Before proceeding into the execution phase of your change project, make sure your sponsor and the entire change team are committed to the depth and breadth of what it will take to make your change a reality. Assess the risks of reducing or eliminating the components that you and your communities deemed necessary to ensure success of the change:

- Will you still be able to achieve the business outcomes in the timeframe expected?

- What effect will scaling back have on impacted employees' willingness to participate in the change?

- Will modifying the plan re-introduce "gotchas" that caused previous change initiatives to fail?

Recap of the Technique

In order to be sure that your employees have everything they need to be successful and that you have removed all possible barriers to adoption, ask the following questions:

- Have you communicated everything that people need to know about the change?

- Have you given them all the necessary tools to be successful?

- Have you been very clear on what it is you expect them to do?

- Have you provided a forum for them to give you feedback?

- Have you trained them to be successful adopters of the change?

17 DEPLOY, MONITOR, AND ADJUST
THE CHANGE

Explanation of the Technique

For change to be successful, it needs to be actively managed, guided, evaluated, and nurtured. wHolistic Change℠ recommends communicating progress and successes along with honest statements about bumps in the road and adjustments needed.

As you deploy the change based on your plan, recognize that all change efforts have an inherent element of evolution in them. The change will in fact change along the way, with some elements gaining momentum and catching on faster than others. Other elements will need to be reconfigured as you go.

As things evolve, pay attention to what is winning. "Survival of the fittest" should mean survival of the best options for advancing your organization toward its goal. An interesting thing can happen, though. What if the element that evolves and wants to survive doesn't really appear to be advancing toward the stated organizational goal?

It could mean that the stated goal of your change effort (change message) might merit a revisit. Have the benefits been defined correctly and realistically? Is the goal really beneficial to your organization? Does the fall-out of getting to the goal leave bodies along the wayside as you go?

Figure 50. As you deploy, measure progress against your definition of success to determine if you need to adjust your plan.

We're not saying that bodies along the wayside can always be avoided. However, be aware of the survival instinct that will cause people to cling to what they know and try to evolve the change back to what is comfortable for them.

It could also mean that your stated goal needs revisiting because the newly evolving element is better than where you were originally headed. The collective intelligence of your change team and the feedback of the organization may have identified a better answer.

If it's a minor adjustment, this may not take long. Bigger shifts may mean that you really need to go back to the beginning to analyze stakeholder impacts and put together a new change plan.

When your change changes, it can be very hard on your sponsor, champions, and change agents. These individuals have been on board and are moving you forward toward an understood vision, and now they need to shift gears. You'll need to bring them back together, lay out what's different, and get their commitment and buy-in again.

How easy this will be will depend on much your change has "morphed":

- Take a deep breath, because this can be a very emotional scenario. Instituting a change doesn't come lightly. If change happens at all, it's because there are passionate and dedicated people who are committed to making it happen.

- Figure out if what you were trying to do still makes sense within the future landscape that just got repainted. If it does, then this could actually be a good thing for your effort. If what overtook you is broader, has better sponsorship, or has more resources, then see if your change team can become part of the larger team and work on a coordinated effort.

- If your change no longer makes sense, then you'll need to dismantle your change team. Pay special attention to your champions and change agents when you're doing this. Change is hard, and un-changing the change is also hard. Make sure that members of the team are recognized for their contributions, even though they will not get to see the effort through to the end.

- If the new proposed change runs counter to what you are trying to achieve and your goal is still valid, then it's time to start advocating for what you see as a necessary future. You may have an opportunity to influence the direction of the other effort so that you're back in alignment.

If you recognize that change is evolutionary, staying open to it will keep your organization nimble and give you a better chance of survival. When your plans change, you will need to communicate so that everybody impacted understands the new vision. Make sure that all components of the services, people, process, and technology changes are aligned to the new vision.

Why Is This Step Important? What Happens if You Skip It?

Plans can go awry at any time—when you are implementing a large, transformational change; when there is a natural disaster; or just in the normal course of business if your suppliers cannot keep up with demand. When this happens, be sensitive to how your customers perceive your response to the challenge.

If your reaction is one of compassion for your customers and if it demonstrates an understanding of the impact of the issue on their plans, you may preserve your business reputation despite the temporary inconvenience for everybody involved.

If your response, however, seems more inwardly focused on your company's bottom line or is oblivious to your customers' concerns, you will have to do a lot of work (that is, costly damage control) to try to regain credibility and trust.

Things can also fall apart when there are too many things changing at once. How do you recognize when there is too much change?

Here are a few key signs:

The change message has become fragmented. When you hear people talk about what is changing, you start to hear many different points—all of which are actually part of the change effort. Yet there are so many different points that people are only absorbing part of the big picture. People don't understand how what they know might actually fit into the big picture.

Focus is lost. People can no longer really tell you what the purpose and reason for the change is. You get different answers depending on whom you ask. This could also be an indication of an ineffective communication plan. In that case, you'll have to put some thought into whether or not that might actually be the issue.

Everything is a top priority. Everybody knows that the change effort is important, but there are so many things that need attention—everything seems to be critical. In this scenario, people become overloaded and can no longer be effective change agents because they have to spread themselves too thin to try to address everything that's urgent.

Key alignment communication falls apart. When there is too much change happening, when the change requires key alignment people to work with you to figure things out yet you see less and less time devoted to key alignment communication because everybody is too busy, this is an indication that you're overloaded.

When the pace of change is too fast for people to keep up and the scope of what they are being asked to do isn't feasible within the timeframe expected, your change agents and change team members will not have time to be thoughtful and to see things through to completion. Change is hard,

119

yet it doesn't have to result in burnout.

Recognize when there is too much change—or when your business environment has changed—and adjust your plan.

Checklist

#	Deploy, Monitor, and Adjust the Change Reporting
1	Change objective: What you set out to accomplish (from Chapter 9, "Develop the Change Message").
2	Measurement of success: How you defined change in terms of business value and how you are doing against those goals (from Chapter 3, "Define Success").
3	Change road map: The high-level picture showing the stages of services, people, process, and technology changes (from Chapter 13, "Create the Change Road Map"). Include not only the change that the team is driving, but also all of the services, people, process, and technology changes happening simultaneous to or in conjunction with this organizational change: • Creating this picture provides an opportunity for the various change teams to coordinate communications, training, and any implementations that would best be done together. • The road map can also minimize disruptions to the business by not unintentionally bombarding your employees with multiple demands for achieving different certifications or behavior changes in too short a period of time to be successful.
4	Key milestones: Planned completion dates for key change deliverables (from Chapter 12, "Develop the Deployment Strategy"). We have found that color-coding the milestones gives a nice at-a-glance visual to your sponsor and Communities of Practice. This way they will know what is done, what is yet to come, and what needs help to get it back on track: • Green: on track • Yellow: at risk • Red: off track • Blue: complete
5	Success stories. Because there will be a large percentage of people in your organization who will be reluctant to adopt your change, it is critical that you regularly communicate and celebrate your successes: • What has worked really well? • What beneficial changes have you already seen through the deployment of your change to date? • What customer delight stories have you heard?
6	Critical issues and risks, including resolution plans and timing

Figure 51. Deploy, monitor, and adjust the change reporting checklist.

Decision Point: Proceed from Execute into Operate?

Once the business objectives are met, the sponsor and the change team manager need to decide when to consider the change execution phase as complete. At that time they will disband the change team and ensure that all materials are handed over to the operational owner(s), who will maintain the change as part of ongoing business as usual.

Before proceeding into the operation phase of your change, make sure your sponsor and the owner(s) are committed to the continuous improvement process. This will ensure that the business benefits gained to date are not lost after the project is completed.

Recap of the Technique

As you roll out the change, reinforce your message by celebrating your successes. What are your customers saying about the change? What positive impacts have you seen?

Remember to put the change in the context of overall change happening in the organization and in the customer community to help make the impact of the change "real" to your target audience.

When parts of the deployment strategy fail, it is important to be honest about them. This will build credibility in the eyes of your sponsor as well as throughout the organization. Not every item on your deployment strategy will go as planned. Provide reporting to manage expectations throughout the change process about what has changed and what still needs to happen.

Be honest about the issues that have come up and your plans for remediation. This will establish credibility on behalf of the change team, which in turn will foster trust in the people who are impacted by your change.

18 COMPLETE THE CHANGE: TRANSITION TO OPERATIONS

Explanation of the Technique

The change is now business as usual. Congratulations! wHolistic Change℠ makes sure that the change is now embedded in the organization through:

1. Defined vision
2. Established sponsorship
3. Established leadership
4. Defined authority
5. Established key alignments

Once these are achieved, the change team will be disbanded and all materials will be handed over to the operational owners (continuous improvement team) to maintain the change. These owners will monitor the continuous improvement suggestions to make future tweaks to the services, people, process, and technology solutions, as needed.

Figure 52. After the change is deployed, hand it off to an owner to maintain the change as business as usual.

1. Defined vision
It was the change team's responsibility to define the future state vision and—through the communication plan and other activities—to drive and establish the future state. Even if the vision was not shared across the organization, it was commonly understood with enough sponsorship to drive the change.

When you make the transition to operations, do what you can to guarantee that the defined vision will remain intact. One way to accomplish this is to have established sponsorship.

2. Established sponsorship
As part of the change effort itself, sponsorship was crucial to success. Equally important is sponsorship for the ongoing continuous improvement. When the excitement and angst of the change have calmed down and what was new is now every day, it is very easy for things to slide backward or sideways. It will be the diligence of the continuous improvement team and their governance that will keep things on track.

Sponsorship is needed to ensure that the continuous improvement team has the resources—people, funding, hardware, software, physical workspaces—and credentials behind them to continue to have a voice that will be listened to within the organization. The voice of the continuous improvement team is heard as a result of having established leadership.

3. Established leadership
The structure of the continuous improvement team can take multiple forms: a Community of Practice, a self-selected committee representing various interests, or a set of appointed representatives, among others.

No matter how the group is structured, there will need to be some element of leadership defined, however loosely. Ask yourself:

- Who will convene the continuous improvement team?
- Where and how often will it meet?
- Who will be the point of contact when a question or suggestion for improvement needs to be brought to the team?

For the leadership and the continuous improvement team to be effective, they need defined authority.

4. Defined authority
The continuous improvement team will need to know what their span of control is. When the group is established, clearly define what the team will be empowered to do. Do they have the authority to make decisions and take action to make future improvements? If yes, is it broad authority? Or is it only within a defined boundary?

The connection the continuous improvement team will have with sponsorship needs to be established. Even if the team is given broad authority to act, they still need to communicate up. A sponsor can't act as a sponsor if she doesn't know what is happening. Ongoing, defined channels of communication need to be established with the sponsor.

Along with sponsorship, defined channels of communication need to be set up with the team's established key alignments.

5. Established key alignments
When the change build-out is done, all of the mutually beneficial change initiatives that you worked with to drive the change are probably the same teams with whom you will need to stay connected. It's very likely that the key alignments will need to participate in any continuous improvements.

At the point of transition to the continuous improvement team, identify named individuals from each of the key alignments. Then set up a plan to reach out to them periodically and tell them what you've been doing. Proactive communication outward may result in information back from the key alignments regarding changes they are making in which you have an interest.

If the items we discussed are solidly in place, a change team can feel confident that they can walk away knowing the continuous improvement team has been set up for success.

Why Is This Step Important? What Happens if You Skip It?

In order to guarantee that the success lasts, create the structure that will ensure that the change continues to be part of how you do business, even after the change team has been disbanded.

A lack of resources—people, funding, hardware, software, and physical workspaces—to maintain the change is one of the biggest pitfalls that you can run into.

There's a certain amount of excitement and energy—fully recognizing that it could be negative energy—that comes with something new and different. In general, everybody "gets" that it takes resources to move things from point A to point B. Once you're at point B, then why should it take any resources to keep you at point B? I mean, really … you're there … how could it not stick?

Ongoing continuous improvement resource allocation is what will keep point B alive, meaningful, and adaptable to changes coming in the future.

You developed relationships with the mutually beneficial key alignment change initiatives during the change effort. If you don't have any people assigned to stay connected with them, you could be blindsided when they propose a change that is not optimal to your newly established day-to-day business operations.

In this scenario, you end up expending resources to try to adjust and reposition what that new change is asking for in order to keep your business operations on track. This is panic mode. It might have actually been more cost effective to allocate individuals to stay connected in the first place, as well as be at the table representing your interests and needs.

Keeping resources allocated to continuous improvement means that you have a named person that anybody within your organization can go to with an idea or a suggestion for improvement.

If you don't have that clarity and a defined channel for suggestions, how will somebody with a good idea get that communicated to somebody who will pay attention? If you have a resourceful employee, she'll find a way. On the other hand, somebody who still has a great idea and is a little intimidated by crossing business units or approaching management may never get her idea across.

In the long run, it really is more cost effective to keep continuous improvement alive and funded, with named individuals. Otherwise, you may lose out on some great ideas and opportunities and therefore be constantly in reactive instead of proactive mode.

Checklist

As your change nears the point of becoming operational, include these key components in the transition plan from the change team to the operational owner, who will continue to run the business going forward:

#	Transition Planning from Change Team to Owner(s)
1	Has the owner been trained to take over the change? • In the event that your training and development plan includes certifications, the owner will need to be well-enough versed even if not fully certified to ensure that she understands how the changed business runs from a services, people, process, and technology perspective. • Because the owner will be responsible for the ongoing maintenance of the change, the owner will need the skill sets outlined in Chapter 10, "Train the Change Team." If the owner did not attend training earlier, determine if she needs training on any of the skills that an effective change agent needs to ensure continued adoption and maturation of the change.
2	Does the owner understand which components of the change are negotiable, as well as which, if any, are not negotiable? • Change takes time. The owner will continue to encounter resistance until the organization has completely adopted the change. This can take years. • If a key component of your case for change included specific deliverables, the owner needs to be made aware of these as well as the rationale for why they are immutable. Or if not, why the deliverables are not immutable.

#	Transition Planning from Change Team to Owner(s)
3	Does the owner understand her role as an owner of the change? A key component of maintaining the change and continuing the change momentum is ensuring that the execution of the change continues: • The owner must govern the specific change within her purview. • The owner is responsible for the end-to-end governance of the change's impacts to upstream and downstream owners.
4	Does the owner understand the other owners with whom she needs to remain aligned going forward? If the owner has not yet been introduced to the other players, now is the time to schedule individual meetings to begin to establish the relationships. Starting topics should include: • Who the key stakeholders are from each vertical and horizontal span of control. • How each owner views the success of the initiative. • What each owner will need from one another to make this happen. • Any "gotchas" that each should be aware of. • The preferred mechanism to resolve conflicts that will arise, such as email, a phone call, or in-person regular meetings.
5	Does the owner understand the continuous improvement process and her role in the process? • The owner will need to understand the closed loop feedback process. • The owner will also need to be comfortable facilitating any tweaks to the services, people, process, and technology as they arise.

#	Transition Planning from Change Team to Owner(s)
6	Is the owner prepared to continue to manage the communication plan, going forward? Since the change team established the communication plan for all impacted stakeholders, it will be imperative for the owner to know what communications need to continue: <ul><li>Who needs to know?</li><li>What do they care about? Why is this important to them? The messages will need to be pertinent and impactful for the receiving parties.</li><li>Where will they feel the change? What is the impact to their aspect of the business?</li><li>How frequently do they expect communications?</li><li>Why are the continued changes needed?</li><li>What mechanism will be used to communicate?</li><li>How are success stories gathered? If the change team had established a particular mechanism or if it had stockpiled some voice-of-the-customer feedback, this will be invaluable to help the owner with her first communications.</li><li>How long before the owner can expect to develop her own positive change stories? Depending on her previous involvement in the change, it may take some time for the owner to compile her own examples of the benefits of the change.</li></ul>
7	Is the owner familiar with the defined success metrics? <ul><li>Does the owner have the tools to continue to measure progress? "Tools" could be any combination of services, people, process, and/or technology that generate data to demonstrate continued improvement in terms of delivering business value.</li><li>Is the owner familiar with any skill-set assessments to be able to gauge whether there are ongoing training needs?</li></ul>

#	Transition Planning from Change Team to Owner(s)
8	Has the owner met the Communities of Practice? Does the owner understand the value of nurturing these communities? • By definition, a Community of Practice is a group of people who come together to share information and knowledge and to achieve a defined purpose. • As your change becomes operational, some of the Communities of Practice will dissolve; for example, a community who came together to create the templates for a new process will likely no longer need to meet once the templates have become a standard part of their daily jobs. • Some of the communities' purposes may evolve from having been a group of subject matter experts interested in piloting your change to becoming a more formal governance structure for managing the change going forward. • It will be up to the owner to help the CoPs take stock of where everybody is on the change road map and to help determine what the structure should look like going forward. Regardless of what decision the owner and communities make, the front-line employees will still be the best source for understanding how decisions affect your customers and, thus, the bottom line.

#	Transition Planning from Change Team to Owner(s)
9	When will the formal handoff from the change team to the owner be considered complete? • If the change team was made up of employees—or if the team included consultants who will be retained to work on another initiative within your organization—it is imperative that the owner and the change team set a hard deadline for when the owner will become the central point of contact within the organization. The changing of the guard needs to be communicated to the entire stakeholder list. • From the owner's perspective, she will only really become comfortable answering questions and feeling fully responsible for the change once it has been officially handed off. • From the change team's perspective, the goal of the project was to implement change. In order for it to be truly considered a success, the change team should be dissolved and the people should be redeployed on other initiatives within the organization. • From the stakeholders' perspective, the owner will establish her credibility and authority as the owner when she becomes the go-to person for any questions, concerns, and sharing of success stories.

Figure 53. Transition planning checklist.

Recap of the Technique

Create a solid transition plan to turn the measurement and maintenance of the change over to one or more operational owners. This ensures that someone will be accountable to continue to deliver the business objective that your organization just invested so much time, effort, and money to achieve.

Here's how you make sure your change is now embedded in the organization:

1. Defined vision
2. Established sponsorship
3. Established leadership
4. Defined authority
5. Established key alignments

If organizations don't have a solid transition plan, they can lose the momentum for continuing to improve. Even worse, they can lose the business benefits that were achieved while the change team actively monitored the organization's progress.

19 CONCLUSION

Your employees are your best chance for the future.

Their ideas, contributions, and satisfaction will drive your success. Involve them, listen to them, and tell them what they are doing right. Above all, thank them.

This kind of feedback tells your employees that you value them and it helps to build a workforce that is happy to come to work every day. They are your brand ambassadors—from the first contact your customers will have with your receptionist down to the quality of the product that is built on your production lines.

When it is time to change how your organization does business, utilize the wHolistic Change℠ approach to define the change, determine what your employees need to be successful, and then coach and guide them through the change while ensuring that they have clear lines of communication to tell you what is working—and what is not.

We promise that if you follow the approach we have laid out in this book, you will be on your way to delivering a corporate change that lasts!

20 GNATS, A CASE STUDY

This case study is a fictitious example of how the principles behind wHolistic Change℠ have been applied to effect change. Be aware that there have been many liberties taken here. In addition, we have kept the breadth of the case study fairly limited. We hope that you'll take this example in a light-hearted spirit and that you'll enjoy it.

Make the Case for Change

The National Park Service is charged with preserving and caring for the nation's historical treasures. The most recent National Park Service inspection of the Lincoln Memorial found significant deterioration of the memorial surface.

The National Park Service determined that the rate of deterioration was due to frequent washing of the memorial to remove an excess of bird droppings. The National Mall and Memorial Parks Management had experimented with different detergents and brushes to cut down on the wear to the memorial. The real problem was how often the memorial needed to be cleaned.

Figure 54. The Lincoln Memorial.

To ensure that the Lincoln Memorial is available for the enjoyment of future generations, the National Park Service decided that it needed to make a change.

#	Question	Clarifying Commentary	Stakeholder Response
1	What is the business problem or opportunity?	Stakeholder need or concern	The surface of the Lincoln Memorial was deteriorating due to frequent washing.
2	Who is asking for change?	Stakeholders (internal and external)	National Park Service
3	Why #1	Why is change important? Why is the problem happening?	Why was the memorial being washed so often? To remove all the pigeon guano.
4	Why #2	Why …?	Why were there so many pigeons? The pigeons ate the large number of spiders.
5	Why #3	Why …?	Why were there so many spiders? The spiders ate the high number of gnats.
6	Why #4	Why …?	Why were there so many gnats? The gnats were attracted to the lights on the memorial.
7	Why #5	What is the heart, or true systemic cause, of the business problem or opportunity?	Why were there more gnats at the Lincoln Memorial than at other sites? Traditionally, the lights at the Lincoln Memorial have been turned on at sunset, while the lights at other memorials are turned on an hour after sunset.
8	How will change benefit the stakeholder?	What's in it for them?	Turning the lights on at the Lincoln Memorial an hour after sunset will reduce the gnats, spiders, and pigeons and thus the need for frequent washing with harsh detergents. This will preserve the memorial.

Figure 55. Five whys case for change worksheet for the Lincoln Memorial.

Define Success

If turning the lights on later achieves the desired change, the Lincoln Memorial will need to be cleaned less frequently. Less frequent washing will result in a slowed rate of deterioration.

The Lincoln Memorial attracts millions of tourists each year. The primary success metric will be based on the interval of cleaning frequency. At the same time, Park Rangers and the Public Relations Department will pay attention to visitor feedback on the amount of bird droppings on the monument.

#	Question	Clarifying Commentary	Stakeholder Response
1	What is the business problem or opportunity?	Business driver for change	The surface of the Lincoln Memorial was deteriorating due to frequent washing.
2	Who is asking for change?	Stakeholders (internal and external)	National Park Service
3	What is the vision?	How will the business look after the change?	The Lincoln Memorial is being cleaned less often. Tourists will not report a degradation in cleanliness of the Lincoln Memorial.
4	How will success be measured?	Measurement	a. The frequency of cleaning the Lincoln Memorial b. Visitor feedback
5		Mechanism to measure the change	a. Annual National Mall and Memorial Parks maintenance report b. Monthly visitor feedback survey card responses

#	Question	Clarifying Commentary	Stakeholder Response
6	What will change look like after it is implemented?	Current state	a. The memorial is being cleaned every three months b. Seasonally adjusted 30 visitor complaints per month regarding bird droppings
7		Future state goal	a. The memorial will be cleaned every six months b. Seasonally adjusted 30 visitor complaints per month regarding bird droppings
8		Timing when future state is expected to be achieved	Year-end 2013

Figure 56. Define success metrics for the Lincoln Memorial.

Obtain a Sponsor

Jo Swanson, Vice President of the Preservation Department of the National Park Service, is the executive sponsor. Jo has successfully implemented preservation efforts for other national monuments and is a member of the National Park Service Executive Leadership Team. She will be able to advocate for this change and for all resources the gnats project change team needs—people, funding, hardware, and software.

Identify All Stakeholders

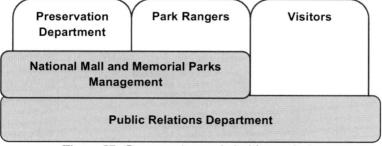

Figure 57. Gnats project stakeholder analysis.

The Preservation Department is tasked with ensuring that the Lincoln Memorial continues to exist as an historic site for future generations.

Park Rangers answer questions daily from visitors to the Lincoln Memorial.

Visitors travel to the Lincoln Memorial to behold its majestic appearance and to celebrate our nation's history.

The National Mall and Memorial Parks Management is responsible for the signs, maps, and maintenance of the Lincoln Memorial.

The Public Relations Department manages Lincoln Memorial visitor feedback surveys and publishes the survey results to all departments within the National Park Service.

Assemble the Change Team

Name	Role	Stakeholder
Jo Swanson	Sponsor	Preservation Department
Alice Andrews	Subject matter expert	Preservation Department
John Johnson	Owner	Park Rangers
Ryan Roberts	Change agent	Park Rangers
Sally Smith	Owner	National Mall and Memorial Parks Management
Judy Carpenter	Change team manager	National Mall and Memorial Parks Management
Jenny Jones	Change agent	National Mall and Memorial Parks Management
Brenda Jackson	Owner	Public Relations Department
Sam Jung	Communicator	Public Relations Department

Figure 58. Gnats project change team.

The National Mall and Memorial Parks Management will provide the budget and change team manager to shepherd the change. The Public Relations Department will develop and manage communications about the change in illumination hours. The Public Relations Department will provide Visitor feedback to the rest of the change team.

Perform Current State Analysis

Services	People
• The National Park Service is dedicated to preserving our nation's historic sites. • Visitors may access the Lincoln Memorial 24 hours a day. • Park Rangers answer questions daily about the memorial. • The Lincoln Memorial's lights turn on at sunset and off at sunrise. • The surface of the memorial is cleaned every three months. • Public Relations Department manages visitor feedback surveys—survey development, analysis, and dissemination of results to all departments within the National Park Service on a monthly basis.	• Preservation Department reviews National Park Service historic monuments for signs of deterioration. • Public Relations Department handles all communications to the public regarding hours and access to the monument. • Park Rangers staff the memorial. • National Mall and Memorial Parks Management schedules lighting in and around the memorial. • National Mall and Memorial Parks Management performs the cleaning of the Lincoln Memorial. • Public Relations Department communicates feedback from the public to the National Park Service.
Process • National Mall and Memorial Parks Management standard operating procedures indicate that the Lincoln Memorial is illuminated from sunset to sunrise daily. • National Mall and Memorial Parks Management pigeon dropping removal process requires brushes and GuanoBGone cleanser.	**Technology** • An automated timer system is used to turn the lights on and off at the Lincoln Memorial. The system adjusts the time for illumination based on the sunrise and sunset calendar for Washington, D.C. • National Mall and Memorial Parks Management cleaning schedule indicates pigeon dropping removal once every three months at the Lincoln Memorial.

Figure 59. Gnats project current state analysis.

Perform Future State Analysis
The goal of this change is to reduce the rate of deterioration of the Lincoln Memorial. The hours of illumination and frequency of cleaning will change. Yet the majority of the services and roles at the National Park Service will not change in the future state.

Services	People
• The National Park Service is dedicated to preserving our nation's historic sites.	• Preservation Department reviews National Park Service historic monuments for signs of deterioration.
• Visitors may access the Lincoln Memorial 24 hours a day.	• Public Relations Department handles all communications to the public regarding hours and access to the monument.
• Park Rangers answer questions daily about the memorial.	
• The Lincoln Memorial's lights turn on one hour after sunset and off at sunrise.	• Park Rangers staff the memorial.
• The surface of the memorial is cleaned every six months.	• National Mall and Memorial Parks Management schedules lighting in and around the memorial.
• Public Relations Department manages visitor feedback surveys—survey development, analysis, and dissemination of results to all departments within the National Park Service on a monthly basis.	• National Mall and Memorial Parks Management performs the cleaning of the Lincoln Memorial.
	• Public Relations Department communicates feedback from the public to the National Park Service.

Process	Technology
• National Mall and Memorial Parks Management standard operating procedures indicate that the Lincoln Memorial is illuminated from one hour after sunset to sunrise daily. • National Mall and Memorial Parks Management pigeon dropping removal process requires brushes and GuanoBGone cleanser.	• The automated timer system is programmed to turn the Lincoln Memorial lights on one hour after sunset and off at sunrise. The system adjusts the time for illumination based on the sunrise and sunset calendar for Washington, D.C. • National Mall and Memorial Parks Management cleaning schedule indicates pigeon dropping removal once every six months at the Lincoln Memorial.

Figure 60. Gnats project future state analysis.

Decide on Achievable, Relevant Change

Letter	SMART Goal Questions
S	Specific: Is the goal clear and unambiguous? The goal is to reduce the deterioration of the Lincoln Memorial.
M	Measurable: How will we concretely measure progress? We will quantify the frequency of cleaning the memorial while ensuring that monthly tourists complaints about bird guano do not increase.
A	Achievable: Do we know how the goal can be accomplished? We will reprogram the automated timer system to turn lights on one hour later than the lights turn on today.
R	Relevant: Does this goal matter to our organization? In 1916, President Woodrow Wilson approved legislation creating the National Park Service. The act made the bureau responsible for the U.S. Interior Department's national parks and monuments. The National Park Service is directed to manage and conserve natural and historic objects and to provide for the enjoyment of the same by such means as will leave them unimpaired for the enjoyment of future generations. This change will preserve one of the National Parks' historic treasures: the Lincoln Memorial.
T	Time-bound: What is the target date when change is expected? The change will be made by December 6, 2013.

Figure 61. SMART questionnaire to test whether the gnats project change is relevant and achievable.

Develop the Change Message

Overall Vision Statement

The National Park Service holds preservation to be one of our most important missions. To that end, beginning in December 2013, we are adjusting the evening hours of lighting on the Lincoln Memorial to start one hour after sunset.

Turning the lights on one hour later will reduce the quantity of inserts that are attracted to the Lincoln Memorial. Fewer insects will mean fewer bird droppings that require the National Mall and Memorial Park Management to scrub the historic site to keep it presentable for all who visit and work there. Less frequent cleaning will ensure that the Lincoln Memorial continues to exist for the enjoyment of future generations.

Services Change	Who is Impacted?	Who is Making Sure the Change Happens?
The Lincoln Memorial's lights will turn on one hour after sunset and off at sunrise.	• Visitors • Park Rangers • National Mall and Memorial Parks Management • Public Relations Department	• Preservation Department • National Mall and Memorial Parks Management
The surface of the memorial is cleaned every six months instead of every three months.	• Park Rangers • National Mall and Memorial Parks Management • Public Relations Department	• Preservation Department • National Mall and Memorial Parks Management

People Change	Who is Impacted?	Who is Making Sure the Change Happens?
All Lincoln Memorial staff who interact with the public need to be able to explain the change in illumination hours.	• Public Relations Department • Park Rangers • National Mall and Memorial Parks Management	• Public Relations Department
All Lincoln Memorial staff who maintain the memorial need to be aware of the changed schedule for cleaning.	• National Mall and Memorial Parks Management	• National Mall and Memorial Parks Management • Public Relations Department
The public needs to be informed about the change in the illumination schedule for the Lincoln Memorial and the reason for the change.	• Visitors	• Public Relations Department

Process Change	Who is Impacted?	Who is Making Sure the Change Happens?
National Mall and Memorial Parks Management standard operating procedures must be updated to indicate that the Lincoln Memorial is illuminated from one hour after sunset to sunrise daily.	• National Mall and Memorial Parks Management	• National Mall and Memorial Parks Management

Technology Change	Who is Impacted?	Who is Making Sure the Change Happens?
The automated timer system needs to be programmed to turn the Lincoln Memorial lights on one hour after sunset and off at sunrise.	• National Mall and Memorial Parks Management	• National Mall and Memorial Parks Management
National Mall and Memorial Parks Management cleaning schedule will be revised to conduct pigeon dropping removal once every six months at the Lincoln Memorial.	• National Mall and Memorial Parks Management	• National Mall and Memorial Parks Management
In September 2013, the National Park Service website will announce the upcoming change in illuminated hours for the Lincoln Memorial.	• Visitors • Park Rangers	• Public Relations Department
On the go-live date in December 2013, the Lincoln Memorial page on the National Park Service website will be updated to indicate the new lighting times.	• Visitors • Park Rangers	• Public Relations Department

Technology Change	Who is Impacted?	Who is Making Sure the Change Happens?
A Frequently Asked Questions (FAQ) will be added to the Lincoln Memorial page on the National Park Service website to explain why the hours of illumination were changed.	• Visitors • Park Rangers	• Public Relations Department

Figure 62. Gnats project change message showing vision, change impacts, and who is responsible for making sure the change happens.

Train the Change Team
In order to prepare to solve the deterioration problem at the Lincoln Memorial, the gnats project change team attended a brainstorming class. The training session taught the team to withhold judgment and to welcome unusual ideas to solve problems.

The five whys case for change worksheet showed the root cause of the problem was gnats that were attracted to the lights at the memorial. Brainstorming training enabled the stakeholder representatives to agree on reduced hours of illumination at the Lincoln Memorial as the best solution to the problem.

Here are some other ideas that were generated during brainstorming:

- Put a net around the Lincoln Memorial to stop birds from flying in.
- Spray the monument with an insecticide to repel insects.
- Hose the memorial off every night to reduce the accumulation of guano.
- Turn the lights off altogether. Use only natural lighting.
- Enclose the Lincoln Memorial in a large glass dome.

Handle Resistance to Change

The change team reviewed the ways to reduce resistance to change. Judy Carpenter, the change team manager, incorporated the traits of successful changes into the gnats project change plan.

#	Successful Change Characteristic	How the Gnats Project Change Team is Addressing This Characteristic
1	There is a clear message and everybody knows the reason the change is being made	The change message is a unifying statement that explains why the hours of illumination are changing. The message is being shared with all impacted stakeholders.
2	Life does not get harder as a result of the change	The National Mall and Memorial Parks Management jobs did not get harder or more complex.
3	The outcome of the change is valued and desirable	The rationale for the change ties directly to the National Park Service mission statement: Conserve historic objects and leave them unimpaired for the enjoyment of future generations.
4	The change is nimble and able to be continuously improved	The Public Relations Department will actively monitor tourist feedback to ensure that there is no increase in complaints about bird guano. Park Rangers and the Public Relations Department will report negative feedback to the sponsor, Jo Swanson.
5	Employee incentives are aligned with the change outcomes	There is no conflict between the reduced frequency of cleaning the memorial and how the National Mall and Memorial Parks Management annual performance, bonuses, and promotions are decided.
6	There are constant communications about the change	There is a defined communication plan that is actively being executed by the Public Relations Department.
7	The change team is not burned out at the end of the project	The change team manager will survey whether members of the change team want to play active roles on future change initiatives.

Figure 63. Gnats project approach to handle resistance to change.

Develop the Deployment Strategy

Prior to making the change, the Public Relations Department will conduct a three-month public awareness campaign about the changing hours of illumination at the Lincoln Memorial. The goal is to reduce an increase in calls to the National Park Service Public Relations Department from people who will want to know why the Lincoln Memorial lighting hours have changed.

The public awareness campaign will inform all impacted stakeholders why the change is being made:

- Share the change message with all employees of the National Park Service.
- Explain to Park Rangers how to answer questions from Visitors about why the lighting hours have changed.
- Notify Visitors planning trips to the Lincoln Memorial.
- Inform residents in and around Washington, D.C. about the change.

The communications to all impacted stakeholders will begin on September 3, 2013. The change will be implemented on December 6, 2013.

Create the Change Road Map

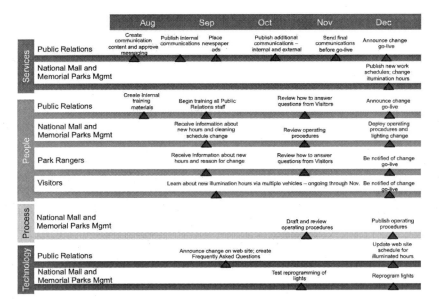

Figure 64. Gnats project change road map.

The gnats project change road map was created by Judy Carpenter, the change team manager, to drive common understanding and a sense of commitment for what is about to happen.

The National Park Service is engaged in an effort to reduce the costs of operating and maintaining the national historic sites without sacrificing the integrity of the sites themselves. The change in hours of lighting the Lincoln Memorial will benefit the National Park Service in ways beyond reducing the deterioration of the monument:

- Provide an energy usage savings by requiring one less hour of electricity to light the memorial 365 days a year.
- Extend the life of the light bulbs used to light the Lincoln Memorial. Light bulb lifespans are quoted based on the number of hours of lighting. Reducing the light bulb usage by one hour each night will extend the time between light bulb replacements.
- Reduce the amount of GuanoBGone cleanser and cleaning brushes purchased each year. Less frequent cleaning will require fewer supplies to maintain the memorial.
- Cut the labor cost of cleaning the Lincoln Memorial in half.

The illumination change may cause a potential public safety impact between sunset and one hour after sunset. The Washington, D.C., police department will be informed so they can plan for any change in police officer patrolling that they deem necessary.

Build the Communication Plan

#	Communication Plan
1	Awareness: Ensure that absolutely everybody impacted by the change is aware of what is happening, why, when, what it means for her, and how she can get involved and/or learn more. National Park Service internal departments: • Share the change message in National Park Service all employee monthly emails—September, October, and November 2013 • Post the change message on the National Park Service intranet notice board—September 2013 • Develop Arrowhead quarterly newsletter feature article, "The Gnats!"—October 2013 • Announce the deployment of the change to all employees of the National Park Service—December 6, 2013 Visitors: • Publish National Park Service Lincoln Memorial website announcement and Frequently Asked Questions—September 2013 • Generate ads in newspapers that cover the Washington, D.C., geographical area—September, October, and November 2013 • Send press release for Lincoln Memorial hours of illumination change—December 5, 2013 • Update National Park Service Lincoln Memorial website hours of illumination—December 6, 2013

#	Communication Plan
2	Understanding: Ensure that the people whose roles are affected by the change understand what it means to them. Park Rangers:<ul><li>Train Lincoln Memorial Park Rangers on new lighting hours and reason for the change—September 2013</li><li>Speak about the change at the Park Ranger quarterly all hands meeting—October 2013</li><li>Review how to answer questions about the change—November 2013</li></ul>National Mall and Memorial Parks Management:<ul><li>Train leadership on new lighting hours, reason for the change, and cleaning schedule impact—September 2013</li><li>Develop cleaning crew manager talking points—September 2013</li><li>Speak at National Mall and Memorial Parks Management quarterly all hands meeting—October 2013</li><li>Post details on the National Mall and Memorial Parks Management intranet notice board—September, October, November, and December 2013</li></ul>Public Relations Department:<ul><li>Train Public Relations Department on new lighting hours, reason for the change, and communication mechanisms being used to inform everybody who is impacted—September 2013</li><li>Update customer service knowledge database to ensure that customer service representatives have information to answer questions about the lighting change—September 2013</li></ul>

#	Communication Plan
3	Adoption: Ensure that the people whose services, roles, processes, and technology are directly affected by the change behave differently. Park Rangers: • Attend a tour at the Lincoln Memorial after the change has been deployed. Alice Andrews will play the part of a tourist and ask the Park Rangers on duty about the changed hours of illumination. She will report back to the change team whether Park Rangers answer questions correctly about the change—December 9, 2013 National Mall and Memorial Parks Management: • Revise standard operating procedures—December 2013 • Update cleaning schedule to every six months—December 2013 • Adjust automated timer to turn lights on one hour after sunset and off at sunrise—December 6, 2013

#	Communication Plan
4	Mentoring: Identify specific people to achieve a level of competence in the change such that these individuals can act as coaches or trainers to others within the organization. Park Rangers (Ryan Roberts, change agent): • Conduct training with all Lincoln Memorial Park Rangers how to answer questions from the public about the change— September through December 2013 • Work on the evening when the change goes into effect. Provide feedback to the change team if Park Rangers encounter a question they cannot answer—December 6, 2013 National Mall and Memorial Parks Management (Jenny Jones, change agent): • Act as the point person to respond to departmental phone calls or email questions as they arise—September through December 2013 • Publish the revised standard operating procedures and cleaning schedule—December 2013 Public Relations Department (Sam Jung, communicator): • Create communications according to the change plan—August through December 2013 • Develop training materials for all impacted stakeholders: Park Rangers, National Mall and Memorial Parks Management, Public Relations Department—September 2013 • Update communications and training materials based on stakeholder feedback or concerns—September through December 2013

Figure 65. Gnats project communication plan.

Establish a Change That Lasts

Each stakeholder identified an employee to monitor the effect of the change in hours of illumination of the Lincoln Memorial on her impacted business unit.

• Jo Swanson is the executive sponsor and representative for the Preservation Department.
• Ryan Roberts is the change agent for the Park Rangers.
• Jenny Jones is the change agent for the National Mall and Memorial Parks Management.

- Sam Jung is the communicator who is representing both the Public Relations Department and Visitors. Sam will also interface with the Washington, D.C. police department with regards to the change.

As the communication plan is executed, the named individuals will actively solicit feedback from people in their respective business units. The stakeholder representatives will email questions or ideas for improvement to the change team manager, Judy Carpenter. Judy will share the suggestions with the rest of the gnats project change team during the weekly project status call.

As the executive sponsor, Jo Swanson makes the final decision whether to make changes based on continuous improvement feedback.

- If continuous improvement recommendations are approved, Sam will update the relevant communications and training materials. He will disseminate the revised materials and inform the change team when the task is complete.
- If continuous improvement suggestions are not approved, Jo will provide the rationale why the feedback change is denied. The stakeholder representative will communicate the denial and reasoning to the person who submitted the suggestion.

Determine Training and Development Needs

The Public Relations Department will develop the National Park Service internal training for the stakeholders impacted by the gnats project:

- Train Lincoln Memorial Park Rangers on new lighting hours, reason for the change, and how to answer questions from the public about the change.
- Educate National Mall and Memorial Parks Management on new lighting hours, reason for the change, and the revised cleaning schedule.
- Teach Public Relations Department about the new lighting hours at the Lincoln memorial, reason for the change, and communication mechanisms being used to inform everybody who is impacted: National Park Service website, newspaper ads, Arrowhead quarterly newsletter, employee emails, and departmental intranets.
- Provide information to the Public Relations Department customer service knowledge database to ensure that call center agents can answer questions about the lighting hours change.

National Mall and Memorial Parks Management will ensure that behavior changes stick at the Lincoln Memorial:

- Revise standard operating procedures regarding hours of illumination.
- Update cleaning schedule to every six months.
- Adjust automated timer to turn lights on one hour after sunset and off at sunrise.

Ryan Roberts will act as a mentor for the Lincoln Memorial Park Rangers:

- Train the Park Rangers how to answer questions from the public about the change.
- Be available to support Park Rangers during the month of December 2013.

The Preservation Department gathers data annually on the integrity of the Lincoln Memorial. The condition of the historic monument will be evaluated in 2014 and 2015 to determine if the gnats project successfully achieved a reduced rate of deterioration.

Deploy, Monitor, and Adjust the Change

The Public Relations Department analyzes visitor feedback surveys and disseminates the survey results to all departments within the National Park Service. The owner of Public Relations, Brenda Jackson, will monitor if there is an increase in seasonally adjusted visitor complaints about bird droppings at the Lincoln Memorial from December 2013 to December 2014. Brenda will share the monthly survey results with the gnats project change team.

Starting in August 2013, Judy Carpenter will facilitate weekly change team meetings to track progress against the project plan and to review continuous improvement feedback. Judy will produce weekly status reports until the end of December 2013.

In January 2014, the gnats project change team meetings will reduce in frequency to monthly. Jo Swanson will decide by the end of January 2014, when to consider the change execution phase as complete. At project completion the change team will disband and hand maintenance over to the operational owner who will maintain the change as part of ongoing business as usual.

Complete the Change: Transition to Operations

Sally Smith, the owner of National Mall and Memorial Parks Management, was identified as the ongoing operational owner of the changes made by the gnats project change team. As the owner, Sally will:

- Maintain the illumination schedule of the lights on the Lincoln Memorial to start one hour after sunset.
- Ensure that the memorial is cleaned every six months.
- Review the monthly survey results from the Public Relations Department for indications of public concern about the cleanliness of the Lincoln Memorial.
- Become the point person to communicate with the Washington, D.C. police department about any safety concerns based on the hours of illumination of the monument.
- Reach out to Jo Swanson to review the results of the annual Preservation Department inspection of the integrity of the Lincoln Memorial in 2014 and 2015.

Sally will bring the gnats project change team back together in the event that either of the following occurs:

- A cleaning schedule of every six months is insufficient to maintain the appearance of the memorial.
- Seasonally adjusted visitor complaints regarding bird droppings exceed 30 per month.

The National Park Service Preservation Department will continue to explore other options to minimize the impact of cleaning on the Lincoln Memorial's surface. The Preservation Department will test the efficacy of new cleaners, as they become available, on the removal of bird droppings and the impact on deterioration of historic monuments.

Conclusion

We hope that this case study gives you a better understanding of the wHolistic Change℠ approach so you will have the confidence to tackle change yourself.

CONSULTED REFERENCES

We are both avid readers and have business book libraries in our offices that we utilize regularly, based on the situation.

Here are a few of the books we have found to be valuable in developing the wHolistic Change℠ approach:

- Deming, W. Edwards. *Out of the Crisis.* The MIT Press, 2000.

- Gladwell, Malcolm. *The Tipping Point: How Little Things Can Make a Big Difference.* Back Bay Books, 2002.

- Goldsmith, Marshall. *What Got You Here Won't Get You There: How Successful People Become More Successful.* Hyperion, 2007.

- Patterson, Kerry, et al. *Influencer: The Power to Change Anything.* McGraw-Hill, 2008.

- Rogers, Everett M. *Diffusion of Innovations (5th edition).* Free Press, 2003.

- Scholtes, Peter R. *The Leader's Handbook: Making Things Happen, Getting Things Done.* McGraw-Hill, 1998.

- Sweeney, John. *Innovation at the Speed of Laughter: 8 Secrets to World Class Idea Generation.* Aerialist Press, 2004.

ABOUT THE AUTHORS

Michelle Smeby is owner and founder of wHolistic Change, Inc. Michelle has more than 10 years of experience implementing enterprise solutions at Fortune 100 companies. She is a member of the Institute of Electrical and Electronics Engineers (IEEE) and is Six Sigma Green Belt Certified.

Patty Stolpman is co-founder and CFO of TechNIX, Inc. Patty has almost 30 years of experience delivering and coaching Fortune 500 companies to successfully incorporate change. She is a member of the International Institute of Business Analysis (IIBA).

Together, we have 40 years of experience working in Fortune 500 companies where we've been involved in change initiatives. Not only have we experienced corporate change that was directed at us, but we have also executed enterprise-wide corporate change efforts ourselves.

We developed the wHolistic Change℠ approach by learning from the unsuccessful aspects of change that we observed along the way. We fashioned a new approach that we have used to successfully drive changes and exceed expectations: delivering sustainable change in shorter periods of time and with greater-than-expected results.

www.wholistic-change.com